WINNING BODY LANGUAGE, PRESENTING AND SALES SECRETS FOR NON-SALES PROFESSIONALS:

How to Read Prospects, Decode Signals to Close the Deal!

By Chris Gold

CONTENTS

Winning Body Language, Presenting and Sales Secrets for Non-Sales Professionals:

These Leads Are For Closers!	7
Sell to your prospects the way they like to be sold	9
You've got to have a scoreboard!	11
7 Essentials for MASSIVE Sales Success!	14
What is Body Language?	16
Defensive body language	30
Aggressive body language	33
Submissive body language	37
Body Language Tactics For Successful Salespeople	42
Boosting your sales	49
How to boost sales and marketing productivity	53
Top 7 Sales-Boosting Strategies	58
Top 7 Nasty Marketing Strategy Habits to Avoid Curing Recession-Related Aches and Pains	61
Top 7 Tips To Attract New Customers	66
Top 7 Marketing Communications Mistakes Businesses Make	69
Top 10 effective presentation techniques.	75
Essential Presentation Skills	79

1. Use Visual Aids	80
2. Making the presentation memorable	82
3. Achieving your objectives	83
Presentation Skills 2. Rehearsal	85
Presentation Skills 3. The Rule of Three	88
Presentation nerves	91
Here are some presentation tips to make your presentation fly.	99
Presentation hints and tips	103
Closing techniques	106
Objection-handling	142
Objection-handling process	143
LACE	146
Objection Chunking	153
LAARC	158

Winning Body Language, Presenting and Sales Secrets for Non-Sales Professionals:

Want Long-Term Success? Build Your Pipeline!

Most sales are not made on the first call. Often it takes six or seven attempts to even get your foot in the door. The key to sales success is in the follow-up! The best sales professionals master the art of managing their leads through a Customer Relationship Management (CRM) system. Many sales reps will tell you that they are organized and that they have "their own" system but look at their workspace and you'll find that they have paper lists and sticky notes spread all across their desk! You are laughing because you know exactly who I'm talking about. Even worse, there are those who have a database, filled with leads, and they think to themselves, "Hmm, today I'm calling all my no-contacts, or my shoppers, or maybe my past appointments." Day after day, they spend hours calling and sorting through lead statuses hoping to find the needle in the haystack. How many times do you see a new teammate come in and find quick early wins in the first three to six months, and then suddenly fall off the map in discouragement? All too often, and it is misdiagnosed as "the honeymoon period is over," or "the excitement of the new job has worn off."

The manager keeps asking, "How many calls have you made today?" ...and salesperson responds with "I've been blitzing all day and have made 40, 60, 80, 100 calls!" Although blitzing off lists feels productive, it's an illusion. I equate it to jumping in your car and looking for new opportunities by driving around the same city block over and over again. Do you see what I mean by short-term success? Now, I'm not saying that you should never blitz your lead base. There are three instances where you should engage in blitzing strategies.

When You Are Playing "Short-Term" Catch-Up On Those Rare Occasions Where You've Fallen Behind On Your Scheduled Actions:

Most salespeople struggle with Time Management. It becomes

especially difficult when you get on a roll and you are closing a lot of deals back-to-back-to-back. This is one of the most important periods in a sales pipeline management "cycle."

Good pipelines often build up like a roller coaster ascending to peak and then bam the deals start rolling in fast and furious and you are doing everything in your power just to keep up! It is exhilarating until you realize the ride has run its course and you have to start rebuilding again. Great pipelines are always full. The best way to keep your pipeline overflowing is to ensure you keep up with your daily scheduled actions. Always make time for short-term catch-up… even when you are on a roll… a little blitz block can get you back on track.

When Your Daily Scheduled Actions List Is So Small, That You Are Trying To Build A Future Pipeline:

Too often you hear reps say that they are not getting enough leads, or they complain about having a bad territory. In most cases, the reality is a weak pipeline. Some sales reps are lucky to have a corporate strategy that generates warm leads. In this scenario, each rep has new leads assigned to them on a daily or weekly basis… but, most sales reps have to generate their own leads.

In either case, the key to successful pipeline building comes in the process of adding new leads to your CRM every single day. Although each sales job is different, a solid goal example would be to build your database up between 150 and 300 new prospects per year. This size lead base would allow you to have a minimum of 20 daily scheduled actions in your CRM.

If you don't have that many scheduled follow-up calls in your pipeline, you know it's time to start blitzing. Always blitz with one goal in mind… "I'm looking for new leads to add to my pipeline." Rookies who are building their pipeline from scratch should be shooting for seven to ten new leads to add to their CRM every day. Veterans who have an established database should strive to add at least three to five new leads to their database each day. Within a few months of following this disciplined approach, you'll have a pipeline that is overflowing with opportunity!

When your sales team is blitzing as a team activity or competition for the day:

Sometimes management will see a lull in activity and turn to blitzing as a means of getting a team moving again. Managers will try to create some excitement and spin it as a fun business building activity… while most of the reps are thinking, "Oh my… here we go again… I hate these."

Superstars who live by the two previously mentioned techniques will rarely get excited about team blitzing because high activity levels are already a part of their daily routine. Maintaining perspective is very important in this instance. Be a leader and do what is best for the team. Lead by example, be a team player, and be a catalyst for success! Always remember, your pipeline determines your success. The next time you self-evaluate, ask yourself three questions. How strong is my pipeline? How many leads do I have in my database? How many daily scheduled actions do I have in my CRM?

Sometimes new sales reps will ask their managers "this or that" questions to determine what activities are most important in their job. You may also hear these questions coming from veterans who are struggling to achieve their goals. They are very important questions because they open the lines of communication and create teaching opportunities for developing your people. Here are some examples of these "or" type questions.

Question: "Is it more important that I hit this goal or that goal?"
Answer: "You need to hit all of your goals."

Chris Gold

Question: "Is it more important that I hit my personal goals or that we hit our team goals?"
Answer: "We need to accomplish both."

Question: "Should I focus on quantity or quality?"
Answer: "Let's build your skill-sets so they're not mutually exclusive…you can to both!"

Question: "What is more important… number of dials or actual contacts?"
Answer: "Both!"

Question: "Should I spend more time managing my database, or working to meet my goals?"
Answer: "Managing your database effectively will help you not only meet your goals; it will help you BLOW OUT your goals!"

Question: "Do you want me to go for the quick sale or build a long-term relationship?
Answer: "Let's do both!"

Give Your Prospects a High Five!

The next time you go into a corporate appointment, give it a try. You high five a decision maker by talking to them about...

1. Current Initiatives - "Tell me about your current initiatives regarding..."
2. Goals & Measurements - "What are the most important goals and measurements that you need to exceed to achieve success?"
3. What's working? - "Based on what you are currently doing... what seems to be working the best?"
4. Challenges - "What are you struggling with the most? ...what's not
working?"
5. Apply Features & Benefits - At this point you can begin to tie in the features, benefits, and solutions that your company or product can offer.

One of the most important keys to this 5-step process, is that you are taking your time with each step... probing for further information and clarification.

You must be patient and resist the urge to start offering solutions and pitching your services. Take notes and have a goal to develop the conversation until you have a minimum of 3-5 "target points" that fit into your product offering.

Once you have those targets, you can proceed with statements and questions like, "This has been a great conversation... and I have some ideas. Maybe you and I could come up with some solutions that would help with (state your "target points"). Would you be willing to discuss some ideas and work together on creating some solutions?" Wait for the big "YES"... and begin to tie in the appropriate products, services, features, benefits, etc. to the most applicable "target points!"

Best Practices:

Focus the Client's Goals - Go into every meeting thinking about how you can truly make an impact and help the client be successful.

Let the Client Do the Talking - Make the conversation about their message, not yours. An ideal appointment with a decision maker has you talking mostly about the decision maker's goals and initiatives, and very little about "your company."

Reflect and Clarify - Reflect their message back before beginning your response. An example of this would be, "so what I'm hearing you say is... (reflect & clarify)." It shows the speaker that you are actually listening and taking note the things that are most important to them.

Use Your Probing Skills - Do not monopolize or dominate the discussion. When you are asking questions, you maintain control of yourself, while maintaining control of the conversation. The better your questions, the better the conversation will go, and the less chance of you dominating the conversation.

You've got it... that's the High Five! Your prospects are waiting... Go get 'em!

THESE LEADS ARE FOR CLOSERS!

What are the characteristics of a great closer?

Confidence – Closers have incredible confidence in themselves and in their product. They believe there is no company they can't crack... no deal they can't make. There's no doubt they are offering the right solution at the right price. They know how to create an environment where the customer knows it's time to buy.

Leverage– Closers know how to create value by asking the right questions, uncovering the most pressing needs, and creating urgency to buy now. They have positioned themselves intelligently and leverage everything they've learned about the client's motivation, challenges, and budget. They apply just the right amount of pressure, at just the right time, to make the deal happen.

Opportunity – Closers can see the deal from a mile away. They know how to paint a picture and create a win-win opportunity. They spend their time wisely, with the clients that are most likely to buy.

Strategy– Closers are like chess players. They have the skill and the talent to think three to four moves ahead. Each action builds upon the last... and keenly sets up the next move. They have been executing their strategy right from the start. Everything they say and everything they do has a very specific purpose.

Expertise– Some people have told me this isn't important. I disagree. The best-of-the-best build their expertise. Closers understand the problem, the solution, and the deal… backwards and forwards. Nothing throws them off. Let me put it in perspective. Put two closers head-to-head with the same exact closing skill… the only difference is that one is more of an expert than the other…who wins?

Relentless – Closers are relentless. They are oblivious to stall tactics and unsubstantiated rejection. They build a huge pipeline, with multiple deals waiting to be made… so there is never a sense of panic or desperation. With high integrity and class, they do whatever it takes to make great things happen!

SELL TO YOUR PROSPECTS THE WAY THEY LIKE TO BE SOLD

Lately it seems like the most common approach I have been seeing and hearing about comes in some form of the soft sell. Why is that? Well, I think it's because everyone is worried about being that pushy salesperson who turns people off the minute they start talking. You know that person... the one who sees you as a number rather than a "human being."

I think it's the same reason people use other job titles, like account executive and account manager, rather than putting the word **SALES PROFESSIONAL** in big bold letters on their business card. It's all about relationships, and selling takes time... right? Well, "yes"... and "not necessarily."

Sometimes you just have to go for it! It's about using good judgment and good taste... and knowing where the line is... to ensure you don't cross it. If you are charismatic, highly-skilled, and have the ability to read people, you can be a "hard-core" sales person who is all about the numbers, AND at the same time, cares about people AND cares about matching a high quality solution to the client's needs.

I was talking to a buddy of mine today, and we got to laughing when I told him, "You know what? When I'm the consumer, I don't think the soft sell works on me. I want the salesperson to get straight to the point and **just sell me!**" If I like the opportunity, I'll ask questions and look for the salesperson to provide me with their expertise and recommendations.

The more excited they get me about buying... the more I like the sales rep... the more I want to buy from them! So, here's my point. People who are teaching us to ONLY take the soft-sell approach are basing their advice on their own personal preference.

This is what they like... it's comfortable for them... and guess what... that's OK... when they are the buyer... not the seller! Our greatest success will come with the ability to be flexible and approach each client the way they like to be sold. There are those who like the soft approach, those who want you to get straight to the point, and those who fall somewhere in the middle.

YOU'VE GOT TO HAVE A SCOREBOARD!

Scoreboards and stack rankings are the name of the game. They let you know whether you are winning or losing. They put you in a position to make adjustments and achieve desired results.

Top Gun – Having a visible scoreboard brings out the best in your top performers. They have a mentality of, "I want to know who's winning... I want to know who's got game... I want to be victorious... In fact, ... I don't care about just winning... I want to dominate!"

Important Note: The greatest performers actually want **everyone** on the team to be successful... it's just that they want to be the best-of-the-best-of-the-best! When big numbers go up, it gives everyone an opportunity to see what's possible!

Beat Your Own Best – I like keeping scoreboards in an Excel file with each month tracked on a separate worksheet. It allows me to look back at a month-over-month historical view of performance. I can track individual and team performance for consistency, improvement, and recurring trends. It provides us with benchmarks for what it will take to beat best performances from one month to the next... and gives us the ability to compare the same time frame year-over-year.

Coaching Tool – If I were only allowed one tool to track and coach for sales performance, it would be a carefully crafted scoreboard. The right measurements drive important discussions, feedback, and decisions. You can shape behaviours by rewarding results within the most important measurements. Of course, there will be situations where you have team members who are struggling. A scoreboard allows them no place to hide. It is a reality check. Although the numbers are public, leaders must handle these individual conversations behind closed doors.

Projections – Become a master of the scoreboard, and you'll be an expert in knowing your business. You know you're getting good when your projections are right on target. It allows you to keep your finger on the pulse, plan ahead, and avoid surprises. Let's be up front on this one. Many salespeople can be overly optimistic and give unrealistic projections. A manager who understands the scoreboard inside and out will quickly be able to tell whether or not the "numbers jive."

Team Goals – Create an environment where the scoreboard is not only about individual performance, but also about team performance. Develop a mentality that thrives on a unified effort to accomplish organizational goals. Many people will actually fight longer for the good of the team than they will for their own individual performance.

BEST PRACTICES:

Accuracy is Critical– Make sure the scoreboard is accurate. This is a non-negotiable. You never want to be in a team or individual meeting where you are providing coaching and direction on numbers that are off the mark.

Choose the Right Measurements- This may take some time. Start with a core set of four or five measurements that you know have a direct impact on success. You can build slowly from here. Although you want to create consistency, don't be afraid to change measurements that are not working.

It's Not a Huddle Thing– Don't put your team in a position to huddle up and individually walk up and write numbers on the board. It is a waste of time and it doesn't take long for your team to get bored with this ritual. Have a designated manager or preferably an administrative assistant that broadcasts the updates for everyone to access.

It's a Daily Thing – The scoreboard should be updated and sent out daily. Create an environment where you expect to see the numbers go up every single day. The longer you wait between updates, the more room you allow for your business to run at a slower pace.

Work Ahead– Ensure that the scoreboard represents more than just the current month. I recommend measurements that apply to a minimum of two to three months ahead. This positions you and your team to enter each new month with business already on the board!

7 ESSENTIALS FOR MASSIVE SALES SUCCESS!

Mind: We all know that we produce great results when our thinking is in the right place. It isn't hard to see when things are "headed" south. Flip-it-up and keep your head in the game!

Action: Some people like to "think on things." Mull it over before getting started. It's the top producers that get moving quickly. Champions master the art of thinking while in motion. Sure... some mistakes will happen in the beginning, but in time, it becomes an inevitable force of forward progress!

Strategy: When our mind is in the right place, and we are moving ahead with positive forward action, we quickly begin to understand what works and what doesn't. Combine the things that work with the right resources and build a plan to keep everyone on track.

Season: Develop a belief that you are always "in season." While others base their success on the time of year, you come up with reasons why you can be successful year-round. Use your strategic plan to stay ahead and find yourself at the top month after month... year over year. Remember, your future success depends on what you are doing right now!

Intentional: Everything you do is for a purpose. As you think through your daily activities, your sales process, your follow-up strategies, recognize reasons for why you do it "that way." You will create principles for success that will shape your behaviours and decisions for life.

Vigorous: So much of our success comes from an ability to remain strong through adversity. Ironically, it is also important to remain strong through our victories. In other words, don't lose focus just because you are winning. Impose your will and achieve your goals.

Endurance: True greatness is the ability to succeed over a long period of time. Durability comes with the strength to overcome pain and fatigue. When other people think that your success is temporary... Show them that your MASSIVE success is permanent!

WHAT IS BODY LANGUAGE?

Astonishingly, body language is the most important factor in human communication. Numerous studies have been undertaken in how Western society communicates and the figures do vary slightly though commonly it is stated that a whopping 55% of communication is down to physiology, or body language, 38% to tonality - the way it is said and just 7% down to the words that are actually used! I would guess that great orators like Stephen Fry and Churchill may disagree, but we can all relate to going to a party and for some reason really liking someone and for another reason really not liking someone else, based on nothing but intuitive reasons.

Body language, physiology, unspoken or non-verbal communication (it goes under many guises) plays a fundamentally important part of the way that we interact with every other person. It is like a mirror that tells us what the other person thinks and feels in response to our words or actions. Body language involves gestures, mannerisms, and other bodily signs.

Our ability to use body language in a positive way can be a powerful tool to our overall personality development. It is the unspoken tool to a successful life.

Suggesting Interest

It is important to know if people are interested in what you are saying; particularly in a sales environment, otherwise, you are just wasting your time. Just imagine you are in an important pitch. You are passionate about our products, so you assume that your potential client feels the same way. But are they really interested? Here are some of the movements exhibited by people who are interested in what you are saying:

- They maintain eye contact more than 60% of the time. The more wide-opened the eyes are, the more interested the person is. In fact, a person maintains eye contact more when listening than when talking.
- Their heads are inclined forward.
- They are nodding their heads. Such action means that they're agreeing with you. That means they're attentive and listening.
- Their feet are pointing towards you.
- They smile frequently. But take note, not all smiles convey the same feeling. An oblong smile is not genuine. It is used to show courtesy, but not necessarily happiness or friendliness. The lips are withheld completely back from the upper and lower teeth, forming the oblong shape. This is usually the smile that many people exhibit when they feign to enjoy a lame joke.

Indications That They're More Open to Agree with You

- There are certain hints to indicate if people are more receptive in accepting your ideas. Some of these are:
- Their hands are flat on the table.
- Their palms are open.
- If they're stroking their chin, they're thinking. They may agree with you after careful evaluation.
- Their heads are inclined forward.

- They are nodding their heads.
- Their legs are spaced out from each other.
- They smile frequently.
- They unbutton their jackets. This indicates friendliness and willingness to collaborate with you.
- Their hands are open. This also indicates genuineness.

Indications That They are Thinking

- People think all the time. But different individuals make different body movements based on the type and intensity of their thinking. Some of their actions are written below:
- They're stroking their chin. This means they are assessing the advantages and disadvantages of the proposal/idea being presented.
- They take their glasses off, after which they may either (1) clean them, or (2) put the tip of the frame in their mouth. They are buying themselves some time to think things over. A frame in the mouth would also likely indicate that they need more details and they are willing to listen.
- They are pinching the bridge of the nose most likely with eyes closed. People doing this are engaged in very deep thought. They may be involved in a difficult situation, where they are aware of the consequences that may occur as a result of making crucial decisions.
- They put a palm below the chin, index finger pointed and extended along the cheek, while other fingers placed beneath the mouth. This gesture more likely indicates thoughts that are criticizing or antagonizing other people.

- They walk with the head down and hands behind the back. People who walk this way are probably worried about their problems, and they are thinking of ways to solve them.

Indications That They Are Defensive

- The mouth might keep a secret, but certain gestures could indicate that people are hiding something they don't want others to find out, such as:
- They walk with their hands in their pockets.
- They cross their arms.
- They hide their hands any way they can.

Signals Conveying Excitement or Interest

- You know that you're about to secure the deal when you start to recognise the signs of excitant or interest. Some of the movements made by excited people include:
- They rub their palms against each other.
- They clap their hands.
- Their heads are tilted forward.
- Their cross their fingers (usually comes with the hope that something big or special will happen).

Indications of Boredom

We've all been there! The long, dry, detailed presentation at the end of the long business meeting going into excruciating detail in all of the 117 slides! You notice others are clicking their pen, tapping their feet, and drumming their fingers.

After the meeting, you hear the presenter ask, "Did you enjoy the presentation?" They would say "Definitely!" But you know better. Their actions indicate just how bored they are! Some signals conveyed by people who are bored and disinterested include:

- Head supported by the palm, often accompanied by drooping eyes.
- They show inattentiveness by staring at a blank space (eyes not blinking) or by looking around frequently. They are pulling their ears. This may also signify that they want to interrupt while another person is talking.
- They are clicking a pen non-stop.
- They are tapping their hands or feet.
- They yawn incessantly.
- Their feet or other body parts are pointing to the exit, as if they are very eager to leave.
- They move restlessly in their seats. This could also mean that they are not cozy or at ease, or they might just be exhausted.
- They cross their legs and constantly kick their foot in a very slight motion (particularly done by females).

If you're the one making the presentation and you discerned that your audience are displaying signs of boredom, don't start talking faster or louder. Restrain from such act even if your instinct tells you to do so. Instead, address it and say, "I'm going to take a pause here. I feel that I'm losing your attention. What's up?" Hear what they have to say. You may discover what's actually preventing them from keeping up with you.

Signals Exhibiting Confidence/Authority/Power

Hugely successful people have an aura; an air of unyielding self-confidence. What gives them this air of total confidence?

- They speak with a low-pitched, slow-paced, downward-inflected voice.

- Chin tilted upwards.
- Chest projected outwards.
- They maintain an erect posture, whether standing or sitting.
- When standing their hands are clenched behind the back or placed beside the hips.
- They have a firm handshake, palms pointing downwards.
- They walk solidly with forceful arm swings.
- They 'steeple' their hands by joining the fingertips of both hands together. The higher the hands are elevated, the more confident they are.

Signals Of Agitation or even Anger

- Their fists are clenched.
- Their hands or feet are tapping.
- Their arms are crossed over the chest.
- Their eyes are blinking constantly.
- Collar pulled away from the neck, like letting some air in during a hot day in the summer

Signals Of Nervousness/Tension

Be aware of your body signals during interviews or business meetings that could convey nervousness:

- Your hands or feet are tapping.
- You can feel yourself developing a high-pitched, fast-paced, stuttering voice.
- You find yourself having to often clear their throat.
- Your arms are crossed, gripping your biceps.
- Your legs are crossed while standing.

Signals Made When They Are Doubting/Suspecting You

Here are some clues that may indicate suspicion or doubt in what you're selling:

- They glimpse sideways from the corner of one eye.
- They are rubbing or touching their eyes or ears.
- Their hands are tucked in their pockets.
- Their arms are crossed over the chest.
- Their glasses are dropped to the lower bridge of the nose, with eyes peering over them. This movement may indicate that you are being examined closely (to the point that you get conscious).

There's one act you usually do when you are the one doubting yourself - rubbing or touching your nose. This subconsciously occurs when you are uncertain of how to answer a critical question or when you are concerned of other people's reaction to your answer.

Body Language

Body language is fascinating. People rarely recognize how much information they give off and how noticeable it is to the human eye. Even to the untrained human eye.

I can remember coming home from school as a child after having a tough day and seeing my mother. Instantly she would look at me and ask what the matter was. I know for a fact the majority of the time, I would answer "nothing." However, her keen exploration would soon make me realize that I had a negative attitude.

In sales, it is vitally important to read body language. There are four major areas of body language you need to observe.

1. Eye Contact and Brow Movement
2. Facial Gestures
3. Torso and Arm Behaviour
4. Leg Activity

Eye Contact and Brow Movement

Let's look at Eye Contact and Brow Movement closely. No pun intended of course. While in a seminar a few weeks ago, a participant asked me a question regarding a point I made. After I answered her, I asked the clarifying question, "Does that answer your question?" She answered me with a stuttering "Yes," however, as she answered me her brows were scrunched together demonstrating negative energy. She also glanced away several times rapidly. By noticing her gestures, it was obvious she did not understand me.

Now let's take a look at positive and negative indicators:

Positive Behaviours

-Direct Eye Contact – Interested, likes you
-Smiling Eyes – Is comfortable
-Relaxed Brow – Again comfortable

Negative Behaviours

-Limited or No Eye Contact – Lying, uninterested, too confined, uncomfortable, distraction
-Tension in Brow – Confusion, tension, fear

There may be several reasons why someone is unable to hold eye contact. Now, I'm not talking about staring at someone either. Notice when you are interested how much eye contact you give and why you look away. It can simply be that you are distracted for example a bird flies by and catches your eye.

When people are not able to tell you their honest feelings, they most often cannot hold eye contact. Another reason for loosing someone's eye contact is when you step into someone's personal space (and each of us have a different size boundary); their natural sign is to look away. Check it out for yourself. Test some people (make sure you know them fairly well; you don't want to get bopped on the head for invading personal space): walk toward your friend and see how close you can get before their eyes dart away. Also note that the same person has different boundaries for different people, thus the tighter your friendship usually the closer you are able to get.

You have it in you to recognize these signs easily.

Facial Gestures

Facial Gestures are the second part of body language to read. The most important part of facial gestures is the mouth. Upward turns in the corner of the mouth are often positive signs and downward turns or flat lines demonstrate negative behaviour. Observe the person's lips to see if they are pressed together or relaxed and comfortable. Do they show signs of happiness or signs of discontentment?

The most important thing to understand about reading facial behaviour is that we all have the ability. Most people however never pay close attention to human tendencies and activities. Success in sales requires you to observe human behaviour.

Arm and Torso Movements

The third important factor in reading human body language is monitoring arm and torso movements. Simple rule to remember is: "Closed-off posture usually means close-minded attitude and open posture means exactly what the name eludes, open or willing attitude." I know you are thinking, "Okay, Mr. Genius now that you have told me the obvious what does that mean?"

Closed-Off Posture

- Shoulders hunched forward – lacking interest or feeling inferior

- Rigid Body Posture – anxious, uptight
- Crossed arms – can be just cold or protecting the body
- Tapping Fingers – agitated, anxious, bored
- Fidgeting with hands or objects (i.e., pen) – bored or has something to say

When these signs appear, don't take judgment on yourself or them it's simply time to take a break and see what that person is thinking.

Open Posture

- Leaning forward – interested
- Fingers Interlocked placed behind the head leaving elbows open and armpits exposed – very open to ideas, comfortable
- Mirroring you – likes you and wants to be friendly
- Still – more interested in what you are saying than anything

Leg Activity

The fourth factor to observe is leg activity. Again, this is another area, which is relatively easy to observe once you know what to monitor. Usually negative behaviour is observed through fidgety leg movements. There is no direct correlation between crossed and uncrossed legs. However, if you notice a person has their legs crossed and one of them is bouncing on the other, it probably is anxiety.

Leg activity needs to be observed simultaneously with arm position. If you notice a person is bouncing their legs and their arms are crossed over or their torso is slumped over the buyer most likely is closed-off.
Your success depends upon how well, you can modify your personal behaviour to adapt to situations. And check in with them, STOP talking and ask them what they think.

If you notice a person is closed down you need to focus on one thing. What do you need to do to increase the person's comfort zone?
The easiest way to increase a person's comfort when they are closed-off is to first utilize mirroring.

Mirroring is a technique by which you observe a person's behaviour and then in a subtle way act the same way they are acting. If their arms are crossed over you should sit back relax a little, and then begin to cross your arms.
A psychologist performed a study on mirroring. Two different teachers taught the students a process. One used mirroring the other did not. It was overwhelming that the teacher using mirroring techniques was believed to be much more successful, friendly, and appealing by the students.

So as you look to the future it is going to require that you practice, practice, practice observing people. Remember, reading body language needs to be done carefully. Unlike verbal communication, body language can be rather abstract.

You already have the intuitive skills to learn the art of reading body language. Now you must become more conscious of the subtle signs your prospects and clients give off.

When you notice positive body language keep on track and move in the direction of closure. If negative signs are being sent to you, step back and redefine your objective internally and externally.

To create more positive energy continually reiterate ideas and validate understanding. Review what you discussed with your prospect and validate it by asking clarifying questions. For instance:

Seller: Mrs. Jones we have discussed a variety of things related to project implementation and pricing structures. We will initiate the project on Dec. 1 and it will run for 16 consecutive weeks concluding on March 31. There are 7 consultants scheduled to be on the project alternating with three people available full-time. The estimated investment is $98,235.00. Does this make sense to you?

Buyer: Yes it does!

(Observe body language. Don't just assume because the person said 'yes' it means 'yes'. You have to watch their eye contact, facial gestures for positive signs, torso and arms to make sure they are open, and finally if they have any noticeable fidgety behaviours in their legs or feet. If you determine quickly this is a sincere yes, offer an opportunity for questions. If there is any doubt in your mind address it now before moving forward. Let's take a look at both ideas.)

Noticeable Doubt:

Seller: Mrs. Jones I notice there may be a few things you're not clear on, what issues do I need to explain further?

Believe me in most cases when you observe body language and observe it with true compassion and desire to understand, your intuition won't serve you wrong.

The client or prospect will have some issues, and they will appreciate you recognizing them. Learning how to define issues early on in a relationship forges a happy road to success. Once the person starts to open up to you with concerns resolve those concerns immediately.

Buyer: Well there is a few things regarding…

Seller: (answer all questions and clear up doubt).

Decisive Yes or After You Clear Up Doubt:
Seller: Mrs. Jones, I'd like to open this discussion-up to any questions you may have regarding the finalization of this project.

It is vitally important you pause when you open the floor up to the individual. Any more words out of your mouth will taint the discussion. The power of your questions is not only in the proper delivery of the question, but how well can you shut-up after you ask it.

Remember reading body language is a matter of paying attention.

DEFENSIVE BODY LANGUAGE

When a person is feeling threatened in some ways, they will take defensive body postures.

Defending from attack

The basic defensive body language has a primitive basis and assumes that the other person will physically attack, even when this is highly unlikely.

Covering vital organs and points of vulnerability

In physical defence, the defensive person will automatically tend to cover those parts of the body that could be damaged by an attack.

The chin is held down, covering the neck. The groin is protected with knees together, crossed legs or covering with hands. The arms may be held across the chest or face.

Fending off

Arms may be held out to fend off attacker, possibly straight out or curved to deflect incoming attacks.

Using a barrier

Any physical object may be placed held in front of the person to act as a literal or figurative barrier. This can be a small as a pen or as large as a table. Straddling a reversed chair makes some people comfortable in conversation as they look relaxed whilst feeling defensive.

Barriers can also protect the other person and if I am powerful, I may use a simple barrier to make you feel less defensive. It also means I control the barrier.

Becoming small

One way of defending against attack is to reduce the size of the target. People may thus huddle into a smaller position, keeping their arms and legs in.

Rigidity

Another primitive response is to tense up, making the muscles harder in order to withstand a physical attack.

Rigidity also freezes the body, possibly avoiding movements being noticed or being interpreted as preparing for attack.

Seeking escape

Flicking the eyes from side to side shows that the person is looking for a way out.

Pre-empting attack

Giving in

Pre-empting the attack, the defensive person may reduce the, generally using submissive body language, avoiding looking at the other person, keeping the head down and possibly crouching into a lower body position.

Attacking first

Aggressive body language may also appear, as the person uses 'attack as the best form of defence'. The body may thus be erect, thrust forward and with attacking movements.

Where attack and defence both appear together, there may be conflicting signs appearing together. Thus, the upper body may exhibit aggression whilst the legs are twisted together.

AGGRESSIVE BODY LANGUAGE

A significant cluster of body movements is used to signal aggression.

This is actually quite useful as it is seldom a good idea to get into a fight, even for powerful people. Fighting can hurt you, even though you are pretty certain you will win. In addition, with adults, fighting is often socially unacceptable and aggression through words and body language is all that may ever happen.

Threats

Facial signals

Much aggression can be shown in the face, from disapproving frowns and pursed lips to sneers and full snarls. The eyes can be used to stare and hold the gaze for long period. They may also squint, preventing the other person seeing where you are looking.

Attack signals

When somebody is about to attack, they give visual signal such as clenching of fists ready to strike and lowering and spreading of the body for stability. They are also likely to give anger signs such as redness of the face.

Exposing oneself

Exposing oneself to attack is also a form of aggression. It is saying 'Go on - I dare you. I will still win.' It can include not looking at the other person, crotch displays, relaxing the body, turning away and so on.

Invasion

Invading the space of the other person in some way is an act of aggression that is equivalent to one country invading another.

False friendship

Invasion is often done under the cloak of of familiarity, where you act as if you are being friendly and move into a space reserved for friends, but *without being invited*. This gives the other person a dilemma of whether to repel a 'friendly' advance or to accept dominance of the other.

Approach

When you go inside the comfort zone of others without permission, you are effectively invading their territory. The close you get, the greater your ability to have 'first strike', from which an opponent may not recover.

Touching

Touching the person is another form of invasion. Even touching social touch zones such as arm and back can be aggressive.

Gestures

Insulting gestures

There are many, many gestures that have the primary intent of insulting the other person and hence inciting them to anger and a perhaps unwise battle. Single and double fingers pointed up, arm thrusts; chin tilts and so on are used, although many of these do vary across cultures (which can make for hazardous accidental movements when you are overseas).

Many gestures are sexual in nature, indicating that the other person should go away and fornicate, that you (or someone else) are having sex with their partner, and so on.

Mock attacks

Gestures may include symbolic action that mimics actual attacks, including waving fingers (the beating baton), shaking fists, head-butts, leg-swinging and so on. This is saying 'Here is what I will do to you!'

Physical items may be used as substitutes, for example banging of tables and doors or throwing. Again, this is saying 'This could be you!'

Sudden movements

All of these gestures may be done suddenly, signalling your level of aggression and testing the other person's reactions.

Large gestures

The size of gestures may also be used to signal levels of aggression, from simple finger movements to whole arm sweeps, sometimes even with exaggerated movements of the entire body.

SUBMISSIVE BODY LANGUAGE

A significant cluster of body movements is used to signal fear and readiness to submit.

This is common in animals, where fighting (that could terminally harm each animal) is avoided by displays of aggression or submission.

Body positions

The body in fearful stances is generally closed and may also include additional aspects.

Making the body small

Hunching inwards reduces the size of the body, limiting the potential of being hit and protecting vital areas. In a natural setting, being small may also reduce the chance of being seen. Arms are held in. A crouching position may be taken, even slightly with knees slightly bent. This is approaching the curled-up regressive fetal position.

Motionlessness

By staying still, the chance of being seen is, in a natural setting, reduced (which is why many animals freeze when they are fearful). When exposed, it also reduces the chance of accidentally sending signals which may be interpreted as being aggressive. It also signals submission in that you are ready to be struck and will not fight back.

Head

Head down

Turning the chin and head down protects the vulnerable neck from attack. It also avoids looking the other person in the face (staring is a sign of aggression).

Eyes

Widening the eyes makes you look more like a baby and hence signals your vulnerability.
Looking attentively at the other person shows that you are hanging on their every word.

Mouth

Submissive people smile more at dominant people, but they often smile with the mouth but not with the eyes.

Gestures

Submissive gestures

There are many gestures that have the primary intent of showing submission and that there is no intent to harm the other person. Hands out and palms up shows that no weapons are held and is a common pleading gesture.

Other gestures and actions that indicate tension may indicate the state of fear. This includes hair tugging, face touching and jerky movement. There may also be signs such as whiteness of the face and sweating.

Small gestures

When the submissive person must move, then small gestures are often made. These may be slow to avoid alarming the other person, although tension may make them jerky.

Chris Gold

Floppy language

Method

When you want to *fail* at persuading, one of the best ways is to use floppy language.

Many of us use floppy language without knowing it. Being non-floppy is a good first step to speaking more persuasively.

Preparation

Before you begin, you need to get your beliefs set up to ensure you fail to persuade.
First, you need to put yourself in an inferior position. Everyone else is better than you, of course. their opinions are right and yours is wrong.

This then sets you up to be powerless. Everyone else has power and you, because of your inferiority in all aspects, have none.

Now you can know, in your heart of hearts that you will fail to achieve anything in life. So when you do fail, you can, at least in that respect, be right.

Enactment

When trying to persuade someone, turn on the full force of floppy language. This includes:
- Apologising frequently, for example starting sentences with 'I'm sorry'.
- Mumbling incoherently.

- Broken sentences with pauses, 'um's, 'er's and other signals of uncertainty.
- Letting sentences tail off into nonsensical ramblings.
- Making frequent use of qualifiers that signal uncertainty and willingness to concede.
- Use of submissive body language.
    - *Yes, er, well I thought that you might, if you want to, that is, think a bit about these, um, ideas that I sort of had. I'm sorry if this is a bad time, but I did want to, well, er, let you, um, know that I am trying to help if I can. Er.*

Discussion

The underlying state that causes much floppy language is low self-esteem. If you believe yourself inferior to others, you will verbally place yourself on a lower rung and concede at the earliest opportunity.

Floppy language is not used just by totally weak-willed wimps. In fact, many people who seem very assured and confident let their floppiness slip out from time to time.

Most of us believe we are superior to everyone else (and those that do often have a serious self-esteem problem that they have hidden, even from themselves).

Watch out for little bits of floppiness leaking into your persuasive language. When others are prepared and listening carefully, they may take this as a signal of weakness and use it as a lever. Of course, you can also look for floppiness in others and use it appropriately.

BODY LANGUAGE TACTICS FOR SUCCESSFUL SALESPEOPLE

As a salesperson it's not always what you say that clinches or loses the deal, but how you say it. If you say one thing and give another message with your body, people will ALWAYS believe what your body language over your words. And it gets worse, not only will they believe your body language - they will also assume that they know what it means.

If your words and body language aren't congruent your buyers won't trust you; If you show that you are nervous your buyers won't trust you. If you aren't sure of yourself, they won't be sure of you. You need to be physically and mentally confident for them to have confidence in you.

The easiest way to get your body language to match what you are saying and therefore, get your buyer to believe what you say is... to sell something you really believe in, to know your product, know it is a good deal. Your job is to convey this honestly and match the right product with the right person. If you believe in what you are selling there is a good chance that your potential customers will too. Faking body language is an art that you probably don't have time to perfect unless you are a scam artist. If you don't feel sure about selling something - don't do it!

Where learning about your body does help is for salespeople who are sure of their product, sure it's a good deal, sure they are selling for to the right person or company but aren't sure of their own ability as a salesperson. They tend to get uneasy about closing a deal, or talking about money, and their body language shows this uneasiness and it is perceived as doubt in the sale.

Your body can make it seem you are asking a question or leaving room for negotiation (or doubt):

- by raising your eyebrows
- by the tone of your voice going up at the end of your sentence
- by a slight shoulder shrug
- by turning your palms upwards as you speak
- by a slight holding of your breath after you finish speaking (as if waiting for a question)
- by a tilt of the head to one side or the other
- by pursing your lips

You need to practice the parts of the sale that make you nervous - talking about money gets easier over time, say the amount to yourself over and over until it sounds normal. Compare it to other things until you are comfortable with the amount. Think of it as potatoes rather than currency. Whatever it takes, do it. When you exhibit any sign of nervousness or 'question' after you have mentioned money, your prospect will not trust you in the same way as if you were confident about it. Smile and delight in telling them the price - if you believe they are getting a bargain you are giving them good news, not bad.

Relax when you ask them for their business (I believe you should be closing from the beginning and this step is hardly necessary) but it should be the fun bit. You have a great product or service and you have found the right match for it. Enjoy.

Once you change your mindset you will change your experience. You will spend more time listening than speaking, more time evaluating what your buyer needs and creating a match. More time watching their body language than monitoring your own.

Does Your Body Language Stop A Sales Presentation Before It Starts?

Most everyone knows that the way you dress can influence others. But you can wear the most expensive business suit and still not convey confidence, approachability and, perhaps most importantly -- sincerity. Salespeople are always looking for new ways to make the sale. What they need to do is remember that you can't sell anything before you can sell yourself.

People put out visual signals based on their body language. Often we are not even aware of doing so. These signals include posture, eye contact, gestures, facial expression and other factors. An effective salesperson needs to know how to master the subtle cues of body language before he or she can be successful. Visual signals can make you appear not to be in control and will detract from your overall presentation and the sale.

Posture

Salespeople are always giving presentations -- whether they know it or not. Even if it's a one-on-one meeting with a client or prospect, you are always presenting your ideas, products, or services.

Your posture is an important part of the presentation. Your objective is to be comfortable and controlled. You want your audience -- the client<s> or prospect<s> -- to see you relaxed and comfortable. This puts them at ease as well.

If you tend to sway or rock while speaking, spread your feet about 6 to 8 inches apart, parallel to each other with toes pointed straight ahead. Flex your knees and put your weight on the balls of your feet. Standing in this position will stop any swaying or rocking motion and reduce distracting heel movements. You can move around and return to this position, just don't pace.

Make sure you are standing up straight and are facing your audience head-on. Keep your posture open with arms relaxed and hanging down at your sides. If your hands are clasped firmly in front of you, your feet are crossed, and your body is tight -- you are not exactly exuding confidence. Other "don'ts" include:

- hands on hips -- you look too condescending or parental
- crossed arms -- you are not conveying a look that says, "Let's talk."
- hands crossed in front of you - otherwise known as the "figleaf" stance, this makes you look weak and timid.
- hands joined behind your back -- this stance (the "parade rest") makes you seem like you have no energy
- leaning back in a chair, if seated -- you look like you're ready to pass judgement
- putting your hands in your pockets -- this makes you seem nervous and can result in jingling any change or keys that might be there

The effective salesperson keeps his or hands open. Hold your chin raised, giving you the aura of being in control.

Gestures

Gestures are in important part of your visual picture. They are reinforcements of the words and ideas you are trying to convey. Gestures include hand, arm and head movements.

We all know people who "talk with their hands" -- in some cultures gesticulating a great deal is the norm.

Two gestures to avoid are:
- using a pointed finger -- this makes you look accusatory, even if that wasn't your intent
- fist raising -- this is hostile or threatening

The most effective gestures are spontaneous. They come from what you are thinking and feeling, and help your listeners relate to you and what you are telling them.

When giving a presentation, make sure you vary your gestures. Don't use the same motion over and over again. Audience members will focus on the repeated gesture and not your content. Use your palms and open them out to your audience when gesturing. Move your arm and hand as a single unit, gesturing up and down. When gesturing, always keep your hands and gestures above your waist.

Eye contact

Any career-related manual or book will agree that one of the most important things that someone interviewing for a new job can do is to make contact with his or her interviewer.

The same is true of a salesperson giving a presentation. Even if it's one-on-one, don't be afraid to make eye contact. When you make eye contact, you are relating to your audience, which will help get your message across and possibly close the sale.

If you make eye contact with someone who quickly looks away, try not to directly look into that person's eyes again. In some culture direct eye contact is inappropriate, and some people just feel uncomfortable. If you are giving a presentation to a group of people, the eye contact should be done in an irregular and unpredictable "Z" formation - looking at one person for three to five seconds and then moving on to next face.

The possible problem area with eye contact is if you over do it, and start to stare. In conjunction with making eye contact, you can nod your head occasionally. This also helps connect with your listener.

Facial expressions

There are different variations on it, but the age-old maxim is true: "Your face speaks a thousand words" or "The look on your face speaks volumes."

Be aware of your facial expressions. If possible, look at a mirror each time you are on the phone -- do this for one week. Watch your face when you are talking on the phone.

Be aware of any artificial, unfriendly, or deadpan expressions you may be making. Do you squint, frown, make strange faces? Once you are aware of any expressions you may make, it will be easier to eliminate them. Practice smiling and looking pleasant. That's how you want to look when meeting clients or prospects.

Some facial expression "don'ts" include:
- arching eyebrows -- this makes you seem surprised or questioning
- frowning -- your moodiness will be the only thing the other person remembers
- grimacing -- your prospect will wonder where it hurts

Chris Gold

Salespeople can learn to practice their gestures, posture, eye contact and facial expressions. Doing so can only help improve your sales performance. The bottom line is that it doesn't matter how exciting or innovating your sales pitch is, because your body language speaks louder than words.

BOOSTING YOUR SALES

Here are ten sales-boosting strategies you can implement now:

1. Launch a customer marketing campaign.

Few businesses market to their own customers as well as they could and, consequently, they leave a potential goldmine of opportunity behind. Your customers could be your most valuable resource. Get to know as much as you can about them and update your customer database. If you don't have a database, start one. Send frequent mailings to your customers and give them reasons to come back and do business with you, such as preferred customer offers.

2. Target your best potential customers.

What you learn about your customers can help you target market to your most profitable group of potential customers. Conduct a survey of your current customers to determine their demographics, such as gender, age, income and where they live, then analyse the results. The results of your customer survey can help you select targeted mailing lists or the advertising media that best reaches your most profitable audience.

3. Ask your customers what they want.

Don't assume, ask. By asking your customers and potential customers what they like and dislike about your business specifically as well as about your industry in general, you will be better prepared to give them what they want. You can also use that information to make all of your advertising more effective.

4. Find out what your competitors are up to.

Find out what your competitors are doing and what their ads say they're doing. Take a look at their strengths and weaknesses, then do the same for your business. Figure out what you do better than competitors, make sure it's something customers want, then run with it. Give your customers a reason to do business with you instead of the competition. You don't have to have the lowest price. You do have to provide a compelling reason for customers to choose your business over the competition, and you have to market that reason well.

5. Rewrite your existing print ads with direct-marketing techniques that get results.

Take a look at all of your advertising as if you were a customer. Is it compelling? Does it persuade the customer to do business with your company? Use some of these direct-marketing techniques to improve response:

Create a powerful headline. The headline is the most important part of your ad. It's what stops the readers and gets them to read the rest of your story or not. It doesn't have to be funny, cute or clever. It does have to compel readers to read the ad and take action.

Write your ad copy to sell. Use your ad to tell readers how doing business with you will benefit them. Most companies talk about themselves more than they talk to their audience. People want to know what's in it for me. Make sure you tell them. Include testimonials to boost credibility.

Include a call to action. Tell them exactly what you want them to do: call today; visit our showroom; call for more information; order now. People need to be nudged in the right direction. The right call to action can dramatically improve the results of an ad.

Include a good offer. Give readers a reason to act now. Offer a percentage off, limited-time sale, free gift or valuable information. Be sure the offer has an expiration date, so the reader doesn't procrastinate. Effective ads give people a reason to act now.

6. Expand your Networking Efforts

Get out of the office and meet people. Attend networking events that reach your audience. If you're buried and can't escape, send someone else to represent your company. Follow up with the people you meet.

7. Start a Direct-Mail Program

Start with your own customers and purchase a targeted mailing list that includes your best prospective customers. Create a series of mailing pieces to persuade recipients to do business with you, using the direct-marketing techniques mentioned in this article. Since frequency is the key to success, make sure you create a mailing schedule and stick with it.

8. Launch an Effective Advertising Campaign

Select the media that best targets your audience, then create a campaign using direct-marketing techniques to drive results. Just as in direct mail, frequency pays off.

9. Track Everything

If you're not asking your customers how they heard about you, start. Keep track of exactly when and where your ads ran and which ads they were, then analyse the results. You can discover which media, which target audience, which days, which offers, and which messages generate the best results. You can then re-allocate your budget to maximize your return-on-investment.

10. Improve your Follow-Up

Eighty percent of sales are made on the fifth or later sales call, yet most salespeople give up after two or three attempts. Don't give up! Keep in front of your prospects with mail, phone calls or opt-in email. Be friendly and persistent. By improving your follow-up, you can increase sales from your current stream of prospects.

HOW TO BOOST SALES AND MARKETING PRODUCTIVITY

Much focus and planning are done in the business sector to boost sales and marketing productivity.

There are several ways and techniques through which the sales and marketing productivity can be enhanced. This is not dependent upon the type of investment made, but rather can be contributed to smart planning and strategies which are deployed to boost sales and marketing productivity.

Therefore, a small business can make more sales and run a better and stronger marketing campaign then a big budget business spending millions of dollars on promotions if the small business marketing plans are strong and innovative.

There are several simple ways which can boost sales and marketing productivity which do not require much financial investment and can be easily deployed by small business which do not have the financial potential to support big promotion programs.

Some of the ways are listed below.

Analysing the target market

To properly analyse the target audience of the business greatly helps in boosting sales and marketing productivity. Most business is designed for specific audience and indulging in marketing campaign and promotional expenses which targets all general public regardless of the product significance and use for them is senseless and a waste of profits. Knowing the specific customers and target market for the business on the other hand is very significant as it helps the campaign to focus all its effort on specific customers and devising promotional plans to boost sales and marketing productivity becomes a relatively simple and affordable task if the target market is known.

Making use of Information Technology

Information technology is the fastest growing medium in the world today. If use properly then this medium can be utilized to boost sales and marketing productivity in much faster pace as compare to any landmark promotional campaign. The internet is a medium which is being accessed by millions of people every day and therefore promoting business on the internet via web pages and banner advertisement is a best way to boost sales and increase marketing productivity.

Innovative schemes

To boost the sales and marketing productivity it's not mandatory to do costly advertisement and promotions. The key to success in marketing in the present era is simplicity and originality. Those campaigns which have innovative concepts and the potential to capture the imagination of the customers help in boosting sales and marketing productivity.

Boosting Sales: Become a Problem Solver

Sales representatives are always told, and often in not so subtle terms, to create a sense of urgency in their prospects. After all, you want the potential customer or client to purchase your products and services now rather than at some undetermined time in the future. The problem is with creating that need, on the part of the prospect, to make the purchasing decision right away. The disappointed salesperson is usually faced with the classic responses, "I have to think it over", or "I'll get back to you on it." Should the sales rep agree to the delay, the opportunity for creating that sense of urgency is lost. After all, the prospect believes that purchasing today, next month, or next year are all the same thing based on the sales discussion. The problem often starts with a failure on the part of the seller to listen for the real needs and problems of the potential buyer.

To develop a sense of urgency on the part of the prospect, the sales rep should do less talking and more listening. A canned, rapid fire statement of all the great things your product and services can do for the potential customer, is of little use if their specific requirements are not being met. Let the prospect tell you their problems, and your sales team will soon discover where your goods or services can help.

Have your sales team think as problem solvers, and not salespeople. The many prospective buyers have many different and wide-ranging problems facing their businesses or personal lives. Every person and business is unique, but with careful listening, your sales staff can often craft the right solution, for the individual prospect's difficulties. By listening carefully to the buyer's unique circumstances, that sense of urgency will follow.

When the buyer states the problem, which could range from direct cash losses from lower revenues to higher than necessary expenses cutting their cash flow, your sales rep should listen for the important points. Have the sales representative repeat back the problem in a paraphrased form. By repeating the exact problems back, in the salesperson's own wording, it tells the buyer that your person is listening to their problems.

Since listening is not always practiced in sales, the prospect will start to form a relationship with you or with your representatives. Teach your sales staff to listen more to what the client has to say about their needs or those of their company. Stress problem solving and building relationships, when conducting sales training, rather than the older idea of simply making a sale.

Once the problem has been restated, the buyer will usually continue with even more details. More careful listening, and questions for clarification, will help the prospect understand the importance of acting now. They can see the money they could save or earn in real dollar terms, with a sales rep they feel understands their unique business. After all, the sales rep listened to and was able to fully comprehend the problem.

After the problem is fully understood, then the solution can be offered. At this point, following the full discussion of the entire range of issues and problems, the sales representative has earned the right to offer the appropriate, individually suited solution. Because the listening process uncovered the real problems, the sense of urgency to find an effective solution is created.

Instead of thinking it over, or getting back to your sales representative, the prospect will become a valued customer. A longer-term relationship between your sales staff and their clients will follow as well. People buy from people who they know, trust, and who actually listen to their needs and solve their problems.

Listen first, repeat the important points back in your own words, and help the prospect tailor a solution for their problems. With your sales team turned into problem solvers, your sales revenue will rise, and your customers will be happy to work with your company over the long term.

The sense of urgency is now yours. Create that team of problem solvers within your business right away.

Don't think it over. Do it today.

TOP 7 SALES-BOOSTING STRATEGIES

The competition is fierce and ad budgets are tighter than ever. If you're looking to boost profits and gain market share, there are some things you can do to gain a bigger piece of the pie.

Give your product a distinct personality.

OfficeMax's Rubber-Band Guy is an instantly identifiable, highly memorable character that has boosted sales and brand recognition. It personifies the brand while selling the message that whatever customers need, they can get at OfficeMax.

Give them an interesting history lesson.

Some of the most common products we use today have the most interesting development histories. Hippocrates, the father of modern medicine, left historical records of a powder made from the bark and leaves of the willow tree to help heal headaches, pains and fevers. By 1829, scientists discovered that the silicon in willow plants was the key ingredient in aspirin, which was later repackaged and marketed by Bayer.

Sing your product's praises.

Create a memorable catchy song, poem or jingle that that hooks in people's minds. Gillette sold millions of razor blades using "The Best a Man Can Get," which continues to stick in consumers' heads, leaving a positive impression about the product's unbeatable performance.

Re-package your product for the customer.

Create new convenience packaging that makes your product easier to buy, use or refill. Motor oil used to be sold in cans that required a punch-in can opener or separate punch-through spout. These were messy and troublesome to use. Now oil is sold in twist-open, easy-pour plastic bottles.

Promote product sharing.

This can be done by showing how your product brings friends and family together. An emotional appeal like this can be very memorable. A good example is Almond Joy's, "you can share half and still have a whole." Another is the ubiquitous Friends-and-Family discount, which abounds in everything from cell phones to vacation packages.

Make you product sui generis.

Establish the fact that your product is generically in a class by itself. Consider Porsche's use of the line "there is no substitute." Or products that have become household words: "blow your nose with a Kleenex," or "make me a Xerox copy."

Think outside the demographic box.

Attract a new category of customers by thinking outside the

box. Consider gaining younger or older buyers by expanding the utility and style of your product, e.g., cell phones for 'tweens, or health bars for seniors.

TOP 7 NASTY MARKETING STRATEGY HABITS TO AVOID CURING RECESSION-RELATED ACHES AND PAINS

If you're in marketing, the tell-tale throbbing head and queasy stomach often associated with a hangover just won't go away. Indeed, marketers all over the country are faced with a bottom-line economy in a deep freeze as their consumer and B2B customers opt to hibernate until the forecast improves. We suggest an aggressive avoidance therapy that will yield positive and lasting effects on recession-related aches and pains, not to mention better marketing performance. Here are seven nasty marketing strategy habits that only serve to make matters worse.

Thinking only of yourself... when it comes customer satisfaction

Your efforts to improve customer satisfaction will fall flat if you only concentrate on figuring out how well your brand alone satisfies customers on the things they want from products or services in the category or industry. Not understanding how well a brand is doing relative to your competitors leaves a gaping information hole when it comes to deciding where to allocate limited resources. Say a bank finds out its customers give it an 89% satisfaction rating on "providing accurate statements," but a 75% when it comes to "reasonable ATM fees," the bank would probably focus on fixing the fees. Smart move? Not if its customers gave all its competitors a 98% on accurate statements and 45% on reasonable fees. Considering only your brand may give you absolute numbers, but absolutely no help when it comes to making the marketing investment moves that will pay off the most.

Giving up without much of a fight… when it comes to positioning

Noted authors Al Ries and Jack Trout talked about positioning as the "battle for the mind," but these days most marketers wave the white flag of surrender without putting up much of a fight. We've found that less than 10% of buyers could associate anything with the five leading brands in a wide variety of categories that even remotely resembled a reason-to-buy message (a.k.a. positioning).

Yet a clear, definable positioning can work wonders for marketing performance (not to mention a marketer's career). Consider Skol, a bit player in the Brazilian beer market and barely eking out a profit until, that is, it took up the "smooth flavour" positioning. Today it's the #3 brand in the world—without a drop sold in North America—and its brand manager became CEO of Inbev, the world's largest brewer and the new owners of Anheuser-Busch.

Ignoring what's right in front of you... when it comes to innovation

The next big opportunity in terms of profits AND competitive advantage could be the next version of your current product. Take the case of Dunkin' Donuts, a power brand in New England that a few years ago hoped to expand nationally. At the same time, it worked to develop and test completely NEW store concepts to roll-out into national markets, it also identified what it could proactively change about its EXISTING stores that would boost sales and profitability.

While Krispy Kreme and Starbucks shutter stores around the country and struggle with their brands, Dunkin's recharged configuration of its current stores means it has more resources available to continue to expand and take on the new 800-pound gorilla in the coffee shop category, McDonald's. Getting so wrapped up in finding the next product or service breakthrough that you ignore the product or service right in front of you means you're more likely than not leaving money on the table.

Talking the talk, but not walking the walk... when it comes to integrating marketing communications

It's not exactly a well kept secret that each media channel or "customer touchpoint"—be it advertising, PR, sponsorship, direct, tradeshow, promotions, or the sales force—tends to have its own set of managers and handlers who may or may not tune into (or care) what's going on with everyone else. It's not impossible to scale the walls that separate advertising from PR, promotions from the sales force—it could be as easy as communicating who the key customer targets are for the marketing organization as a WHOLE and more closely monitoring to ensure the sum of the parts haven't gone off on a tangent. If you want to maximize the power of your marketing efforts across communications channels, you have to put maximum effort into getting everyone on the same page.

Leaving media in the dust... when it comes to market segmentation

You may take the time and effort to identify and develop a profile of different market segments to guide product or brand positioning decisions, but when it comes to deciding where and when to communicate with the folks who are in theory most likely to buy your brand, you're left to your own devices to figure out the most efficient media buy. Something is wrong with that picture. In fact, many of the common techniques used to sort buyers do not deliver groups with distinguishably different media preferences and exposure patterns—a pretty big knock against the usability of the segmentation. Whether you have more money to work with or less, you're not going to get the most mileage out of your marketing spend if you don't consider the media decision in your segmentation plans.

Making too many false friends... when it comes to brand loyalty

While it's tempting to believe that "heavy buyers" or "heavy users"—the 20% of customers that account for 70% or even 80% of a brand's sales—are the most loyal and dependable of the lot, this is not always the case. For years, Saks Fifth Avenue put substantial marketing money towards rewarding the folks who spent the most, until, that is, it discovered that they were not exactly monogamous. They were simply fashion-forward, high-powered, wealthy women who spent a lot of money on clothing and spread it around equally to different stores including Saks' competitors Bloomingdale's, Neiman Marcus, and Nordstrom. Saks set to work to find its real friends—the customers with positive attitudes, feelings, and perceptions of Saks' brands, stores, and merchandise—and develop a close relationship with the customers who felt closest to them.

Making much ado about nothing... when it comes to Marketing ROI

The drive towards making marketing more accountable has brought in numbers, numbers, and more numbers, but little in the way of useable performance results. You can show senior management here's what we got on this performance metric, that's true, but you can't say if it's a good number, a bad number, or, very importantly, how to improve the number (and these days senior management is very well going to expect you to be able to do just that). In spite of their plethora, the numbers haven't made it any easier to justify spending, nor offered much in the way of guidance on what's working, what's not, and what to fix. And that's the kind of information CEOs and CFOs need to see and hear about if you want them to take marketing seriously.

TOP 7 TIPS TO ATTRACT NEW CUSTOMERS

Generally, when a company is trying to generate sales leads, using only one tactic is not going to work. You need to mix it up – use traditional techniques like direct mailers along with electronic tactics like sending out e-newsletters.

Here are a few tips to get those sales leads you need:

Buy competent leads.

This is the easiest tactic – rent a reliable prospect list. You can get a mailing list from a variety of sources, including professional organizations, trade groups, and list brokers or alumni associations. These lists give you highly qualified leads (you get to pick most of the qualifications) that you can either mail or email your marketing materials to.

Become an expert.

Join online forums to answer questions or give your expert advice to people in your industry. You can join Web sites that review products or that is just for opinions to up your expert credibility. You can also write articles free for industry Web sites and include a link to your Web site in your byline to drive traffic to your online store. Try to contribute to organizations, Web sites and industry journals so that you can point back to those when customers ask why they should buy from you.

Partner up.

By collaborating with a complementary business, you can share contacts and also share resources. This can lower your marketing costs, such as for colour printing for brochures, which gives you even more flexibility to reach a bigger target market.

Advertise in e-newsletters.

Using electronic media is a great way to generate leads if you have a Web site. It is easy for people to read your ad, and then click on your link to check out your Web site.

Read the local newspaper.

By keeping up with the news, you can pinpoint businesses or individuals who might need your services. For instance, if you read a story about one of your competitors closing its doors, you know this is a great time to send out direct mail pieces on how you will fill the gap left by your competitor.

Attend a trade show.

Try to find a local trade show and pay to set up a booth. Trade shows are a great way to generate leads and to talk with complementary businesses about partnering, which can also increase your leads. Consumers who attend trade shows are there to find information, and you are just the person to give it to them!

Chris Gold

Sign up for a networking organization.

These groups work, plain and simple. What they do is share leads with member businesses that are not your direct competitors. You will have to pay for this information – annual dues are generally hundreds of dollars, but you can generally recoup that cost by contacting the leads you never would have gotten otherwise.

TOP 7 MARKETING COMMUNICATIONS MISTAKES BUSINESSES MAKE

Marketing communications programs work. They help businesses sell their products and services. There's a catch, though. (Isn't there always?) You need to do things right – like define the right audience, follow up with leads, and stick with it!

You can spend a lot of money on these programs, so getting results matters. Here are the top mistakes I see companies make when using marketing communications.

Keeping It A Secret

This seems basic, but many businesspeople either forget the need to get out the word or purposely avoid this step because they're worried about the competition. The usual outcome of not telling the world about your product, service, or company is disappointing sales. Prospective buyers need to know about you and your offering before they'll buy. It's your job to tell them.

Giving Up Too Soon

It can take nine (9!) or more repetitions of a message before it sticks in a prospect's brain. Don't be alarmed if a single ad, mailer or whatever doesn't yield a phenomenal response. Keep at it with consistency, and you'll see results.

Not Using The Power Of The Mix

Repetition is good. But it can be expensive and hard to achieve if you rely on just one communications type. A mix of tactics carrying the same message to the same audience is more effective and affordable.

Not Being Buyer-Oriented

You know what you want to say. But do you know what your prospects want to hear? If you don't know, then ASK! Do some simple research. Prospective buyers pay more attention to messages that speak to their needs.

Being Boring

Truth is, an uninspiring presentation will get through if it's repeated enough times. On the other hand, a fun, intriguing, interesting presentation of the same message will cut through the clutter faster. Why settle for boring?

Not Measuring Results

Some businesspeople think that results measurement isn't possible or is too expensive. This is usually not the case. It can take ingenuity and arm-twisting, but it's very possible to measure inquiry quantity and quality, awareness/preference, and more.

Not Learning From Experience

Marketing communications programs aren't static. They should evolve over time to maximize their ROI. Good programs have feedback loops built in -- try something, look at feedback, tweak what you're doing, and try again.

The communications lesson for the day is "know your audience." If you want your message to be meaningful, you need to understand what's important to prospective buyers of your product or service.

Think you already know what's important to prospective buyers? If you've been working in an industry for a while, you probably have a hunch. And you may be right. But why not ask and confirm your thinking? You'll get your information "straight from the horse's mouth," and you'll avoid relying on assumptions that could prove wrong. Especially for major steps like rethinking your company's direction or introducing a product, I recommend investing in research before gambling with the marketing budget.

There are several ways to get smart about what buyers want. All the best methods involve asking questions.

Focus Groups:

Description: A small group (5-9 people) of qualified participants meets to discuss a topic and/or react to a product or idea. Discussion is led by a moderator who follows an established Discussion Guide. Groups may be observed via one-way mirror and may be audio and/or videotaped.

Advantages: - Provide immediate feedback; can help identify issues; lots of control over who participates; can probe and get clarification.

Disadvantages - Small number of participants means results are qualitative not quantitative; cost; difficulty recruiting participants.

Phone Interviews:

Description: Qualified respondents are contacted by phone and asked a series of standardized questions. Interviews are usually conducted by research professionals. A monetary incentive is offered to participants.

Advantages – Fast turn-around; interviewer can clarify answers and probe for more information; easy to segment participants; can provide quantitative results.

Disadvantages – Cost; difficulty identifying qualified respondents; difficulty getting phone numbers.

In-Person Interviews:

Description: Qualified respondents are asked a series of standardized questions. Interviews are often held at a research facility and are usually conducted by research professionals. A monetary incentive is offered to participants.

Advantages – Fast turn-around; interviewer can clarify answers and probe for more information; easy to segment participants; can provide quantitative results; interviews can be observed confidentially.

Disadvantages – Cost; difficulty identifying qualified respondents; difficulty scheduling interviews.

Earth Mail Surveys:

Description: A standardized questionnaire is sent to qualified participants. An incentive may be offered.

Advantages – Lower cost; can yield quantitative data.

Disadvantages – Results may be unreliable since respondents self-select; difficult to segment participants; slow turn-around; no opportunity to clarify and probe; list and postage costs.

I recommend you have a pro design your questionnaire and research strategy, so you get usable information.

Emailed Surveys:

Description: A standardized questionnaire is emailed to qualified participants. An incentive may be offered.

Advantages – Lower cost; can yield quantitative data.

Disadvantages – Results may be unreliable since respondents self-select; difficult to segment participants; slow turn-around (especially with Earth mail); no opportunity to clarify and probe; difficulty getting fax numbers.

I recommend you have a pro design your questionnaire and research strategy, so you get usable information.

Email And Internet Surveys:

Description: A standardized questionnaire is e-mailed to qualified participants or is posted on an special web site. An incentive may be offered.

Advantages – Lower cost; can yield quantitative data.

Disadvantages – Results may be unreliable since respondents self-select; difficult to segment participants; no opportunity to clarify and probe; difficulty getting email addresses.

Internet and email surveys can save money on postage, but you should have a research pro design your questionnaire and strategy, so you get usable information.

Informal Research

If your budget and audience are small, you may be able to do informal research. Here's what I mean. Think of 3-5 questions that will help pinpoint prospective buyers' hot buttons. Call your top customers and prospects and ask away. You'll have great conversations, and you'll learn something each time you talk to someone. Develop a matrix of everyone's answers to learn even more.

TOP 10 EFFECTIVE PRESENTATION TECHNIQUES.

We have condensed all of the presentation techniques down to the most effective. Here are the Top 10 effective presentation techniques.

1. Use visual aids

Using pictures in your presentations instead of words can double the chances of meeting your objectives.

2. Keep it short and sweet

There is an old adage that said - "No one ever complained of a presentation being too short." Nothing kills a presentation more than going on too long.

There are some college professors who will penalise a short presentation (most lecturers see no problem in droning on), but for most people a shorter presentation is better. Keep your presentation to under 22 minutes if you can.

3. Use the rule of three

A simple technique is that people tend to only remember three things. Work out what the three messages that you want your audience to take away and structure your presentation around them. Use a maximum of three points on a slide.

4. Rehearse

Practice makes for perfect performance. Many experts say that rehearsal is the biggest single thing that you can do to improve your performance. Perform your presentation out loud at least four times. One of these should be in front of a real scary audience. Family, friends or colleagues. Even the dog is better than nothing.

5. Tell stories

All presentations are a type of theatre. Tell stories and anecdotes to help illustrate points. It all helps to make your presentation more effective and memorable.

6. Lose the bullet points - don't put your speaker notes up on the screen

Bullet points are the kiss of death for most presentations. Most people use bullet points as a form of speaker notes. To make your presentation more effective put your speaker notes in your notes and not up on the screen.

7. Video yourself

Set up a video camera and video yourself presenting. You will see all sorts of mistakes that you are making, from how you are standing, if you are jangling keys, to how well your presentation is structured.

8. Know what slide is coming next

You should always know when presenting which slide is coming up next. It sounds very powerful when you say, "On the next slide [Click] you will see...", rather than a period of confusion when the next slide appears.

9. Have a back-up plan

Murphy's law normally applies during a presentation. Technology not working, power cuts, projector blowing a bulb, spilling coffee on your front, not enough power leads, no loudspeakers, presentation displays strangely on the laptop - all of these are things that have happened in presentations that I have given.

Have a back-up plan. Take with you the following items - a printed out set of slides - (you can hold these up to the audience if you need to), a CD or data stick of your presentation, a laptop with your slides on it. Just in case it goes wrong.
Guess what? When you have back-ups - you seldom need to use them.

10. Check out the presentation room

Arrive early and check out the presentation room. If you can

Chris Gold

make sure that you see your slides loaded onto the PC and working on the screen. Work out where you will need to stand.

Do you agree or disagree with any of these effective presentation techniques? Have you have any experiences like this? Add it in to the comments box below.

ESSENTIAL PRESENTATION SKILLS

Here we expose the three essential pieces of information that can make your presentation fly. Most of these are common sense, but you'd be surprised how often they are missed out.

1. USE VISUAL AIDS

One of the most powerful things that you can do to your presentation is to add in visual aids.

Research shows that if you use visual aids you are twice as likely to achieve your objectives.

Ditch the bullet points - use pictures instead.

Why should you use visual aids?

How we take in information during a presentation

Professor Albert Mehrabian did a lot of research into how we take in information during a presentation. He concluded that 55% of the information we take in is visual and only 7% is text.

There are some important conclusions that we can take in from this information

1. Use visuals (pictures, graphs, tables, props) whenever you can
2. In a speech you are only using 38% of the communication medium
3. Ditch the bullet points

2. MAKING THE PRESENTATION MEMORABLE

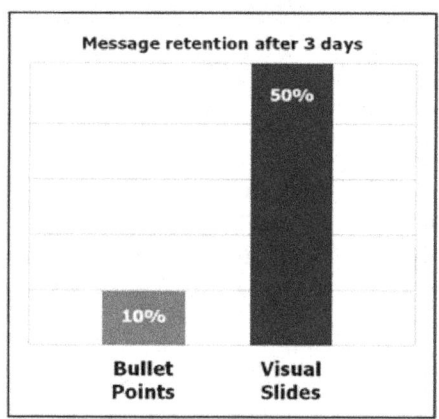

In a Study at the Wharton Research Centre they showed that using visual slides had a dramatic effect on message retention. **The effect of using visuals is truly staggering!**
The old adage that "a picture is worth a thousand words" is as true today as it has always been.

3. ACHIEVING YOUR OBJECTIVES

If I said that I could double your chances of achieving your objectives in a presentation with just one piece of advice you would probably be very sceptical. And yet if you use visual images that is just what happens.

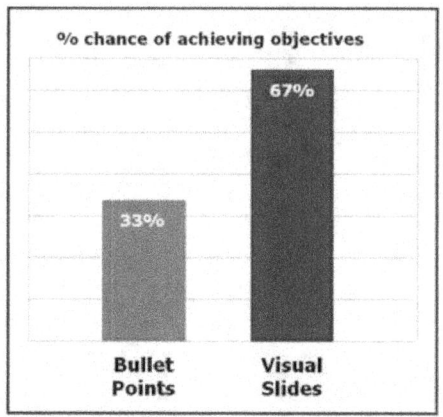

This study by Decker Communications showed that by using visuals in your presentation you could expect roughly to double the chance of achieving your objectives. And if you are trying to make a sales presentation or a job interview presentation, this piece of advice could have a major impact on your bank balance.

The conclusion: Use visual aids. So hopefully by now you have

Chris Gold

got the message loud and clear. Use visual aids in your next presentation.

The old adage is as true now as it has always been.
"If you fail to prepare, you are prepared to fail"

PRESENTATION SKILLS 2. REHEARSAL

We see no end of people who spend hours pouring over their bullet points but fail to rehearse properly for the presentation.

Rehearse your presentation and it will get better.

Sorry to sound like a bit of an old nag. It's obvious - rehearsing - isn't it? But it's also a bit of a drag and one that is easy to forget. It is probably the most common mistake of all presentations that I have seen.

You wouldn't dream of going to see a Shakespeare play at the RSC only to find that they hadn't properly learnt the script. You wouldn't dream of going to the opera to hear the band play out of time because they hadn't got around to rehearsing properly. Yet in presentations and in speeches we see this happening all the time.

Rehearsing could make the difference between a good and an average presentation.

Chris Gold

1. Plan to rehearse your presentation out loud at least 4 times.

We suggest that you should rehearse at least four times, and if you can get word perfect so much the better. I know that you haven't got the time, but we have seen so many presentations that have been let down due to a lack of rehearsal.

Make sure that one of your rehearsals is in front of a really scary audience - family, friends, partners, colleagues; children.

They will tell you quite plainly where you are going wrong - as well as providing you with the support that you need.

2. Rehearse against the clock

If you have to give a presentation in a short period of time, then try to practice your presentation against the clock. This is particularly true with something like the five-minute job presentation. You can add in parts from the script or take them out to fit the time. Allow extra time in your presentation for questions and watch out for nerves - this could mean that you talk faster on the day.

In the actual presentation you could take in a clock or take off your wristwatch and put it on the podium. This way you can see how the timings can develop.

3. Take a leaf out of Winston Churchill's book - memorize your script.

He is widely attributed as being one of the great speakers. It took him six weeks to prepare his Maiden Speech in the House of Commons and he learnt it word perfect.

4. Video or tape record yourself

A very simple trick that could help you with your performance is to video or tape record yourself. This will give you some immediate feedback and will enable you to fine tune your performance.

Videoing a rehearsal is the staple of many presentation training companies - so why not save time and money and do it yourself?

Does it work? - Just read this bit of feedback from someone who got a new job using these techniques

"Then I practised, I think this is the key.
I practised in front of my husband, my brother in law, my 12-year-old daughter.
Then my 4-year-old son on the day, he wasn't impressed, he just wanted me to put the telly on.
I blew their socks off!! he he.
Definitely could not have done it without your help"

Rehearse and you will get better.

PRESENTATION SKILLS 3. THE RULE OF THREE

This is one of the oldest of all the presentation techniques - known about since the time of Aristotle.

People tend to remember lists of three things. Structure your presentation around threes and it will become more memorable.

The Rule of Three - **We remember three things.**

The rule of three is one of the oldest in the book - Aristotle wrote about it in his book Rhetoric. Put simply it is that people tend to easily remember three things.

Remember as a kid when your mum sent you down to the shop to buy a number of things. But when you got to the shop all you could remember were three things. This is the rule of three

Odds are that people will only remember three things from your presentation.

What will they be?

1. The audience are likely to remember only three things from your presentation - plan in advance what these will be.

Believe it or not, the chances are, people will only remember three things from your presentation. So, before you start writing your presentation, plan what your three key messages will be. Once you have these messages, structure the main part of your presentation around these three key themes and look at how they could be better illustrated.

2. There are three parts to your presentation

The beginning, the middle and the end. Start to plan out what you will do in these three parts. The beginning is ideal for an attention grabber or for an ice breaker. The end is great to wrap things up or to end with a grand finale.

3. Use lists of three wherever you can in your presentation

Lists of three have been used from early times up to the present day. They are particularly used by politicians and advertisers who know the value of using the rule of three to sell their ideas.

Veni, Vidi, Vici (I came, I saw, I conquered) - Julius Caesar**
"Friends, Romans, Countrymen lend me your ears" - William Shakespeare
"Our priorities are **Education, Education, Education**" - Tony Blair
A Mars a day helps you to **work, rest and play** - Advertising slogan
Stop, look and listen - Public safety announcement

A classic example of the rule of three was Winston Churchill's famous **Blood, Sweat and Tears** speech. He is widely attributed as saying I can promise you nothing but blood sweat and tears. What he actually said was "I can promise you **Blood, Sweat, Toil and Tears**". Because of the rule of three we simply remember it as Blood sweat and tears.

4. In Presentations "Less is More"

If you have four points to get across - cut one out. They won't remember it anyway. In presentations less really is more. No one ever complained of a presentation being too short.

Presentation Essentials
Three Presentation Essentials:
- Use visual aids where you can
- Rehearse, rehearse, rehearse
- The audience will only remember three messages

So, there you have the presentation essentials. I suggest that you print out this little box and stick it in your workbook for future reference.

So, does it all work? Well it works most of the time - but don't take my word for it Read these **three** posts on the Forum and make up your own mind....

PRESENTATION NERVES

Lose the Fear: Get out there and speak.

You've heard it said many times before - the fear of speaking is considered by many as their number one fear, outdistancing death and divorce. There are legendary stories of entertainment superstars who undergo extraordinary episodes of stage fright immediately before they perform...

They've experienced blurred vision, nausea, and headaches - even after performing hundreds of times. So, if these entertainers face anxiety on stage, is it any wonder that the rest of us may be fearful of appearing before groups? That anxiety may even prevent us from reaching our fullest potential since we may tend to avoid speaking opportunities altogether that could advance our career.

A Learned Skill

While there are many effective methods of relaxation that can help reduce our fear of speaking, the most important step is fundamental. We must begin by recognizing that making presentations is a learned skill. For most of us, it is not something we can simply get up and do effectively without having at least some basic training.

Many executives have unrealistic expectations about their speaking ability, believing that they can achieve proficiency without much effort. This attitude leads to significant frustration when their lax efforts fail to produce the desired results. As one CEO told me during a coaching session, "If I can run a billion-dollar company, then I ought to be able to give a twenty-minute speech without being fearful!"

I address the fear and frustration issues by asking executives, "How many times do you give major presentations each year?" It is usually a small number -perhaps five times. Then I ask, "How often do you make major decisions at the company?" "Practically every day, of course" is the common answer. I respond, "So why do you expect your speaking skills to be as developed as your decision-making ability? You simply do not speak enough to have overcome those fears of public speaking."

Once an executive accepts the fact that it takes time to develop his or her speaking skills, the pressure is off to become a "perfect" speaker. When such a small amount of time is devoted to public speaking, one cannot expect to excel without some coaching and a little practice. Effectiveness is always a reasonable goal even with those executives who don't speak often. But perfection is unrealistic, and impossible.

Take Action: Rehearse and then Rehearse Again

Once you accept the fact that making effective presentations is a learned skill, taking the time to rehearse is a natural step. Rehearsing your presentation over and over again will greatly reduce anxiety. David Peoples, who has trained more than 8,000 IBM salespeople, says, "The single most important thing you can do for sweaty palms is rehearse. The second most important thing you can do for sweaty palms is rehearse. Guess what the third thing is?"

The single most important thing you can do for sweaty palms is rehearse.

The more familiar you become with your material, the more the words flow from you credibly and passionately. The more comfortable you feel with your words, the more naturally you present your speech. That's why good speakers practice - and practice again. Here are two simple ways for you to rehearse your presentation.

Videotape - Nothing will improve your presentation more than seeing yourself on videotape. You will notice mannerisms about yourself that you never noticed before. And you will instantly begin to make changes

Audiotape - Listening to yourself on audio tape is another tool to use when you rehearse your presentations. Immediately, you'll know if you are speaking too quickly, too slowly, or if some words are difficult to understand. You will hear mistakes in grammar and inappropriate "um's" and "ah's" that are quite easily removed from your presentation when you are aware of them. The audio sessions will also help you zero in on content and vocal skills.

Passion Eliminates Fear

Perhaps the quickest way to decrease speech anxiety is to allow the emotion of the subject to fill your heart. Those who speak with passion will most certainly have less anxiety. As speaker

Roxanne Emmerich says, "When you are so committed to the meaning of your message, you can't contain yourself and there is no energy left for being nervous." Now You're Ready!

"The Presentation"

You've just been introduced. You walk to the lectern and are about to say your first words. Wait! You have one more chance to unwind.

Try this: pause for a few seconds and "take in" your audience. Establish eye contact with them. Breathe deeply, smile, and allow yourself to relax for a moment. Now you are ready to begin!

What's the Worst that Could Happen?

In virtually every case, a person's fear of public speaking is unjustified. What's the worst that could happen? You could trip on stage, freeze, forget a sentence, fumble a line, stammer, or shake. None of these is fatal. The worst that could happen probably won't. Yet if it does, you will live through it!

Morton C. Orman, a medical doctor and popular speaker, says, "Even if you pass out, get tongue-tied, or say something stupid during your talk - they won't care! As long as they get something of value, they will be thankful." Ice Breakers

An ice breaker can be a very useful technique to start a presentation or training session. It can either be in the format of a set of PowerPoint slides designed to get the audience interested - or even better, it can allow some form of audience participation. We have collected here a range of ice breakers that you may be able to use at your next presentation or training session.

Ice Breakers

A good ice breaker is where you get people who do not really know each other to get together. Then you give them five minutes to find out two or three things that they have in common (outside of work).
It could be where they were born, where they went to school, somewhere they have been on holiday to, someone they know, hobbies in common.
At the end of the session you get some of them to stand up and say what they have in common. It is amazing how much people really do have in common.

Guess who?

Another technique for breaking the ice with a mid-sized group - it works particularly well in your own company or group - is to ask people to write on a post-it note something about themselves that nobody else would know.

People then have to guess who the answer may apply to. You do not have to do all of the answers - just pick a few at random. You can also save a few for later in the day when people return from a coffee or lunch break.

Some of the answers can be really revealing. One person turned out to have been a breakfast TV presenter earlier in his life and another went into the woods looking for mushrooms!

Story of my life

This involves giving people the chance to make a small book about the story of their life. They have to draw in it a number of scenes about their life. They can play these back to each other or to the group.

Straub test

This was always a good one for a set of PowerPoint slides. Make a selection of PowerPoint slides and ask people to read out the **colour** of the text not just the word it spells. This has become more difficult to do of late due to the popularity of the Nintendo Brain Training game.

Red

Get the audience to do it quickly. They will soon start making mistakes. When they get it wrong you can call out the real colour.

Which finger?

Here is a good one for breaking the ice. Do this to members of your audience in turn.

1. Get your audience to hold out their hands with their arms straight in front of them and their thumbs pointing straight up
2. Ask them to rotate their hands so that their thumbs are pointing downwards
3. Ask them to cross their hands over so that their palms are flat against each other.
4. Get them to interlace their fingers to make a fist.
Now - point to a finger (without touching) and ask them to move it. Now try another. They will probably find the bottom fingers most difficult.
Repeat the exercise with touching - many people find this easier.

Draw a picture

Another ice breaker technique, which is quite simple, is to get members of the audience to draw a picture without showing the other person. They then have to describe the picture to the other person who has to make an exact copy - without being able to see it. All of the instructions have to be made verbally and there can be NO POINTING!

Set a time limit of three minutes.

Most people will find this very difficult. Then allow them a very quick glimpse of the picture. They will then suddenly be able to draw it with ease.

This demonstrates two different learning styles. All too often teachers and coaches rely heavily on verbal communication. Often a picture will help to convey the message far more effectively.

Coincidences

This is an ice breaker that my father (an amateur magician) used to use.

This works well with larger numbers. Ask people to guess how many people you would have to ask before you found two people who have the same birthday. Ask them to call their guess out and write down the answers. Most people think that it will be a number over 100.

Then get people to write down their birthday (just the day and the month) on a big sheet of paper. Get them to call their date out in turn. Write this down on a flip chart. Statistically the average is just 26 people to find a pair that have the same birthday.

You can end by saying, "Isn't that an amazing coincidence. Now talking about coincidences my presentation will now reveal..." and then you are off.

HERE ARE SOME PRESENTATION TIPS TO MAKE YOUR PRESENTATION FLY.

Start with a quotation.

No-one ever complained of a presentation being too short. Long presentations can turn off the audience and be boring. Say what you have to say. Stop and shut up.

A picture is worth a thousand words.

Use pictures instead of bullet points and your message retention should increase. Research suggests that this could be by a factor of five.

Involve the audience.

Happy Computers have made a great success of their coaching business by involving the audience. Their motto seems very apt.
"Tell me and I will forget,
Show me and I will remember,

Involve me and I will understand".
Make the presentation interactive - if you can.

Produce an unusual statistic.

It could help build some connection with the audience. I love the one by Vic Reeves - 93.7% of statistics are made up on the spot. Radio shows are filled with "strange but almost true" quotations.

Live with the fear.

All presenters end up as being very nervous before a presentation - a situation commonly known as "bricking it". We have given literally hundreds and the fear never goes away. It is a combination of adrenaline and testosterone (which affects both men and women). Learn how to harness it, just like an athlete has to.

Realize that you will come down.

I love this quotation from the great performer Robert Houdini that I found in the book - Carter beats the Devil by Glen David Gold.

"It is well known that a magician feels no suffering while on the stage; a species of exaltation suspends all feelings foreign to his part, and hunger, thirst, cold, or heat, even illness itself, is forced to retreat in the presence of this excitement, though it takes revenge afterwards"

When the testosterone wears off, you will come down with a low. If you have done well, you will have been on a high - sometimes known as that Presentation Sensation. Realize that when this goes, often in the evening - you will feel low or even depressed.

No matter how well the presentation goes - you will come down later - usually in the evening. This is only temporary.

Clean your shoes.

You will be on display. Your audience will be looking at how well you are turned out. They will look at your shoes. Make sure that you have cleaned them.

The eyes have it.

Maintain good eye contact with the audience. Don't keep contact with only one group of the audience. Spread your attention around the room.

Avoid jargon.

People really do play buzzword bingo. Whether it is the "TLA" - Three Letter Abbreviation or the "Paradigm Shift" you don't want the audience to be scoring points at your expense.

KISS.

No - not kiss the audience - **K**eep **I**t **S**imple **S**tupid. Reduce your presentation to simple concepts and your audience should be able to follow you. If you go beyond their understanding they will switch off.

Don't use PowerPoint sound effects.

It may seem funny to have applause at the end of a slide, or a screeching sound for a new bullet point, but it will turn off the audience.

Check out the room before your presentation.

Make sure the room has everything that you need and make sure the presentation works on the screen. If possible, go up the day before - or at least an hour beforehand. This will avoid any nasty surprises on the big day.

Don't drink the night before - and certainly don't get drunk.

Alcohol recovery or a hangover will be the kiss of death to your presentation. Alcohol will drain all of the enthusiasm from your voice. And if you've had a drink before you go on, your voice will be slightly slurred. Best avoid it, the time for a drink is after, not before.

Don't lock your knees.

When you get to the lectern, unlock your knees and act as if you were about to catch a ball. It will relax you and make it all flow much more smoothly.

Take a spare tie.

You don't want a gravy spot on your tie before you speak. If you have a meal before you speak take a spare tie with you.

PRESENTATION HINTS AND TIPS

Here are some presentation tips to make your presentation fly.

Write it down

Write down your speech but try not to read from it. If you have written it down - if you dry up, you will be able to pick it back up again.

Put it on tape

When you practice your presentation, do it with a tape recorder or with a video recorder and then play it back to find out which bits sound weak.

Record it

When you speak -try to speak with passion and enthusiasm. If you speak passionately it will make up for many other shortcomings.

Use pauses

Pause - the power of pausing in a presentation can be very profound. It will also give you a chance to catch your breath.

Don't leave it to the last minute

Don't leave it to the very last minute to work on your presentation. When you know you have to give a presentation - make sure that you leave yourself real time to present - and this is more than half a day the night before. You will be standing up in front of a lot of people - you want to to go well. Plan at least 8 hours over the week before.

Prepare the room in advance

Make sure that you have spent time in the presentation room before your presentation. get to know the room and run through your slides beforehand to ensure that everything is working smoothly.

Always leave handouts.

You have gone to a lot of effort to produce your presentation. Leaving handouts will reinforce your messages and will help them to remember your presentation when they look at them again. Always include your contact details so that the audience can contact you.

Memorize your speech.

Do not read from your notes, unless you have frozen or not prepared. It will sound flat and stilted. If you have learnt your speech it will sound natural and you will even have the chance to ad lib, if the opportunity arises.

If you fail to prepare, you prepare to fail.

This is one of the biggest mistakes I see. People think that they can "wing it", but in reality, those who appear to be "winging it" are often very well prepared. Every one of Frankie Howard's muses such as "ooh, now, where was I?" was in the script and well-rehearsed.

It takes more than three weeks to prepare a good impromptu speech. - Mark Twain.

Off the cuff should mean well planned. I once heard a tale about someone who went to the Garrick Club and accidentally left wearing Enoch Powell's coat. In his pocket was a small pile of postcards, with his speech written on them. The speech started with the words "I never expected to be asked to speak this evening!" The professionals do it - so why shouldn't you?

CLOSING TECHNIQUES

One of the most important stages of selling is *closing the deal*, which is the actions taken by the salesperson to gain agreement to the sale. There are many closing techniques in sales, which are prescribed actions that salespeople take to persuade the customer to make the necessary commitment. Here are some of these:

This is a big list, but the real list of closing techniques is almost endless. You can go to each need, for example, and invent several closes around satisfying or threatening them. Here are closing tips to help you further.

'Sell on the tangibles, close on the intangibles' is good general advice. Note how many of these methods follow this rule.

Don't forget the caveat in all of this. If people feel tricked or otherwise betrayed, they will not only not buy from you now, they may well never buy from you ever again or even turn all their friends against you. In particular beware of using unsubtle techniques with professional buyers, who can usually see them coming from miles away.

1-2-3 close

Summarize in sets of three items. We will give you this, that and the other.

This may be features of the product, benefits or add-on sweetener items.

There are two ways to do this: they may either be closely related (to reinforce a single point) or may be quite separate (to gain greater coverage).

Most customers want products that are free, perfect and available now. This is the classic business measurement trilogy of cost, quality and time.

- *This product is cheaper, faster and more reliable than the competition.*
- *The houses here are better-looking, better-built and better-equipped than those on the other development.*
- *If you buy today, we will give you insurance, tax and a full tank of fuel.*

HOW IT WORKS

The 1-2-3 Close works through the principle of triples, a curious pattern where three things given together act as a coherent set of three hammer-blows that give a compelling message.

Adjournment Close

Do not go for the sale now. Give them time to think. Tell them that they probably need time to consider the offer you have made.

Use this when:

- You can see that they are not going to decide now.
- You have set up enough tension that you are reasonably convinced that they will indeed seriously consider the deal and are likely to come back.

- Given some more time, it is likely that they will buy more (for example if they are at the edge of a budgetary period and their current funds are low).
- The relationship is important to you, and them making a wrong decision now would affect the chances of making sales in the future.
- You do not need to make the sale today (for example you have made your quota and this sale would be just fine for next month).

Combine this with setting up the next meeting, when perhaps you will be able to solidly close the deal.

- *This is an important decision for you, and I think you need time to consider how important it is. Shall we discuss the details further next time I see you?*
- *I can see you're thinking very carefully about this. Shall I come back next week to see how you are progressing then?*

HOW IT WORKS

In many sales situations the relationship is very important as the salesperson will be going back to the customer with more sales to make. It is thus a bad idea to push them into a decision when they are not ready and may later be unhappy about this.

Offering an adjournment can be a nice surprise for the customer, who may be expecting a harder style of selling. This sets up an exchange tension, encouraging them to pay back your offer of time with later agreeing to the deal.

The Adjournment Close is particularly easy to manage when the salesperson visits the customer, as opposed to having to hope that they will call back.

Affordable Close

Close out any objections they have about price by making sure they can afford it.

Find how much they can afford. Then show that you have a finance plan that fits their capability to pay.

Bring in other factors to reframe the real price, such as lifetime costs.

Show the price of *not* buying - for example the cost of continued ownership of the current car.

Strip down what is being sold to the bare minimum. Remove all the options (and maybe sell them as separate items).

Sell them something else they can afford.

Last option: bring your price down to what they are prepared to pay.

And always remember the caveat: do not close people into debt they will not be able to repay.

- *How much per month can you afford...yes, we can make a deal for that...*
- *The initial costs seem high, but by the end of the year you will have recouped the costs.*
- *The basic model will fit into your price range.*
- *The maintenance costs on this are very low.*
- *The cost per page of this printer is the lowest in class.*
- *If we can bring the price down to what you say, will you buy today?*

HOW IT WORKS

The Affordable Close works by structuring the finance of the deal to fit into the other person's ability to pay.

'I can't afford it' is often more of an excuse than a real objection.

If they really do not want to buy, you will find that they will immediately jump onto another objection.

Alternative Close

The alternative close works by offering more than one clearly defined alternative to the customer.

The number of alternatives should be very few - two or three is often quite adequate. If you offer too many alternatives, the customer will then be faced with a more complex problem of how they choose between the many alternatives offered.

Note that this technique works well in many different situations where you are seeking agreement, and not just selling products.

An extra technique that can be effective is to add a slight nod when offering the preferred choice. This can be accompanied by subtle verbal emphasis on the words.

- *Would you prefer the red one or the yellow one?*
- *Would you like one packet or two?*
- *Which of these three instruments seems best for you?*
- *Shall we meet next week or the week after?*

HOW IT WORKS

The Alternative Close is a variant on the broader-based Assumptive Close and works primarily through the assumption principle, where you act as if the customer has already decided to buy, and the only question left is which of a limited number of options they should choose.

Artisan Close

In the 'Artisan Close', the salesperson emphasizes the art, skill and ability that has gone into the creation of the product or service that is being sold.

- *This Kitchen Mixer has been designed by skilled engineers and designers who have literally thousands of hours of study behind them.*
- *It may seem like a simple adjustment, but it took three years of training to know how to make the right adjustment.*

HOW IT WORKS

When we are going to buy something, we evaluate it in terms of the work that went into it. If we think it was easy to make, then we value it less. Often, we do not realize the effort and skill required to produce something and hence think it is worth very little.

Selling with the Artisan Close adds perceived value simply by describing the skill of those who made the item and the time spent in producing it.

There is a similar and slightly different effect in service, where the perceived value can be enhanced by explaining the training and skill of those who will be delivering the service.

Assumptive Close

Act *as if* the other person has made the decision already.

Turn the focus of the conversation towards the next level of questions, such as how many they want, when they want it delivered, what size they need, and so on.

- *When shall we deliver it to you?*
- *What will your friends say when they see it?*
- *Will 20 cases be enough?*

- *Where will you put it?*

HOW IT WORKS

The Assumptive Close works by the Assumption principle, where acting confidently as if something is true, it makes it difficult for the other person to deny this. For them to say you are wrong would be to cast themselves as an antisocial naysayer.

Note: This is one of the most common closes used. Many other closes, such as the Alternative Close are variants of the Assumptive Close.

Balance-sheet Close

List both the benefits of the purchase (the pros) and also the costs (the cons). Of course, the pros (the reasons to buy) will win.

You can even write it down like a balance sheet. Make sure the 'pros' column is longer and more impressive, of course.

Cons include things they wanted but are not getting.

Start with the cons and keep them short. But do make it sound credible, as if you are giving them fair consideration.

Then cover the pros. Perhaps sound pleasantly surprised as you describe them.

Sound reasonable, as if you are on their side.

Sound almost as if you are talking to yourself.

- *Well, although it costs this much and is a bit big, it will sound really good and fit well into your house decor.*
- *Let's weigh things up. You're not getting ..., but you are well within your budget and will have ..., ... and .... Hmm. That's good!*

HOW IT WORKS

The Balance-sheet Close works by building Trust through appearing to take a balanced and fair approach. It guides the other person's thinking and hopefully saves them the trouble of weighing up the pros and the cons.

This is also known as the *Abraham Lincoln Close* (Lincoln was a lawyer and often used this technique in his cases) or the *Ben Franklin Close*.

Best-time Close

When people are procrastinating or will 'be back', emphasise how *now* is the *best* time to buy. All salespeople know that 'there are no be backs'.

Invoke seasonal effects, such a Summer, Christmas and other holidays.

Remind them of other short-term reasons, including sales, weather, and so on.

Find out other personal reasons why it is good to buy now, such as their partner's birthday, etc.

You can even do a reversal on 'never the best time to buy' by showing how this makes now as good a time as any.

- *We only bring these into stock for the Christmas season.*
- *Summer is coming. Do you have all the garden furniture you need?*
- *The forecast for next week is for sun. We have limited stocks of sun lotion.*
- *The best time to buy is now, whilst...*
- *There is no 'best time to buy' which makes now the best time.*
- *If you were going to start saving money, when would you*

start?

HOW IT WORKS

The Best-time Close works by emphasising how now is the best time to buy and how delaying is not the best thing to do.

Bonus Close

When they are dithering close to a decision, offer them something unexpected and un-asked for that delights them.

All it needs to do is make them say 'Ooh, that's nice'. Or something like that.

A simple equation: delight = expectation + 1

Try and figure them out before using this close: for some people it will open them up again as they seek to gain more concessions.

- *You know, I've had a good day and am going to give you batteries for free.*
- *Hold onto your money: I'm going to add an extra towel to the pile.*
- *Well, you're a good customer so I won't charge for delivery.*

HOW IT WORKS

The Bonus Close may work in several ways. First, the bonus is a temptation that

When they emotionally close on the bonus, the sensation of closure may also leak across to the main subject.

When they feel they have got something for nothing, they may agree to the deal for fear that you may take it away from them again.

You may also create a sense of exchange, where because you

have given them something.

The Bonus Close is also known as the Delighter Close or the Extra Close.

Bracket Close

Make the other person three offers.

First offer them something sumptuous and expensive that is beyond their budget. Not so far beyond them that they would not consider it. Ideally, it is something they would look at wistfully but just couldn't justify (if they do, it is your lucky day!).

Secondly, offer them a solid good deal that is within their price bracket. It may not have all that they wanted, but it is clearly good value for them.

Finally, offer a severely cut-down deal in which very little of what they want is included.

They should, of course, go for the middle option.

- *you get a full kitchen system with Neff units, brass tops and hand-cut ebony edging. It's a bit pricey but is amazing quality.*
- *A really good option is with Bosch units, hardwood tops and matching edging. This is remarkably good value.*
- *If you are on a very tight budget, we do have some basic units, a nice laminate finish and matching surrounds.*

HOW IT WORKS

The Bracket Close works by contrasting the preferred option both upwards and downwards.

Rejecting the higher option lets the other person feel good about not spending too much. By comparison, the option they choose seems quite prudent and they may even feel they have saved some money.

Rejecting the lower option lets them feel they are not a cheapskate and can afford something of value.

Compliment Close

Be nice to them. Tell them how wonderful they are. Be amazed and impressed by them.
Cast them as the expert so they sell to themselves.
Tell them how good they look or sound.
Tell them how others will be impressed by them.
Tell them how impressed you are with them as a person. Admire their integrity.
Then ask for the sale.

- Also compliment them on previous decisions. If you are selling cars, admire the car they already have, although you can also appreciate their need for a new one.
- *Wow. You really know your stuff. Would you like to buy this now?*
- *Well, as you are the expert, you will understand how good this is.*
- *That dress looks really good on you, madam.*
- *Your friends will be impressed when you show it to them.*

HOW IT WORKS

The Compliment Close works by flattering the other person, massaging their ego so they are more concerned with feeling good than parting with their money.
It can help to associate the person with the product, so they feel their sense of identity becoming attached to the product.
It also works by being nice to the other person, so they feel ob-

liged to be nice to you and buy your product.

Putting the other person on a pedestal and admiring them encourages them to live up to the high expectations you have of them.

Complimenting them on a previous purchase is telling them that they make good decisions (and hence can make a good decision this time too).

The Compliment Close is also known as the Vanity Close, the Ego Close or the Flattery Close.

Concession Close

Offer a concession of something they want in return for them buying the product.

You can be explicit about wanting an order in return for the concession or you can give the concession without asking - the other person will very likely still feel they owe you something for it.

- *If I reduce the price by 10%, will you take the product today?*
- *Well, I think you deserve a free case with this.*
- *Listen, I'm going to throw in a free tank of fuel.*
- *If you are ready now, I'll make sure it is delivered by the end of the day.*

HOW IT WORKS

The Concession Close works by offering the other person something and either requesting or implicitly expecting something in return - usually the sale.

The Concession Close is also called the Trade-off Close.

Conditional Close

When the other person offers an objection, make it a condition of resolving their objection that they make the purchase.

You can also use this approach to make any trade - for example if you want them to watch a promotional video, offer a cup of coffee.

Always, by the way, phrase it in the form 'If I... will you...' rather than 'Will you...if I...'. This is because our brains work very quickly and starting with 'will you' causes them to begin thinking immediately about objections and they may miss the exchange. On the other hand, starting with 'If I...' will cause psychological closure on what you are offering thus drawing them in to the close.

EXAMPLES

- *You say you want a red one. If I can phone up and get you one, will you take it today?*
- *If we can figure out the finance for you, will you choose this one?*
- *If I get you a cup of coffee, would you like to sit down and look through the brochure?*

HOW IT WORKS

The Conditional Close uses the Exchange principle to build a social agreement that if I solve your problem, you will buy the product in return.

Cost of Ownership Close

Do not talk about price. Instead, talk about the total cost of ownership, including service, replacement and so on.

Then compare this cost against that of competing products.

It is often good to scale this price to annual, monthly or weekly cost, where the overall cost may appear scarily high.

- *Competing systems may seem cheaper, but when you take into account installation, maintenance and the lifetime of the product, this system is about half the price!*
- *Because we are so confident about the reliability of our systems, we charge only half the price of our competitors. That means the monthly cost is far less.*
- *If you buy a competing product, you'll be replacing it in two years. This product will last you twice that.*

HOW IT WORKS

People often focus on the immediate price and miss the longer-term cost that may be incurred. The Cost of Ownership Close works by comparing costs over time rather than up-front payments. If possible, this can be put into effect with staged payments.

Of course, you do need a more reliable product if you are going to offer lower service costs. It also helps to have evidence of superior quality.

Courtship Close

Woo the other person like you were wooing a mate. Pay attention to them. Give them sincere compliments. Buy them dinner, if that is appropriate. Put them on a pedestal.

Generally, treat the other person as if you like *them*, as a person, and that selling is a secondary issue.

If the sale is taking place over a period of time, work hard to develop the relationship. Call them often enough to show your interest. Make them welcome when they visit. Be someone who makes them feel special.

The final request for the sale is like proposing marriage to them.

If they truly love you (or at least how you have been treating them), they will, of course, say yes.

- Beware of harassment, stalking and other unwanted attention, of course. You want to attract them, not frighten them away.
- *You know, it's just so wonderful how you look in that coat.*
- *It's so lovely talking to a person like you...No, it's no bother at all...Let me take that for you...Ho ho, you're witty, too...*
- *I have a couple of tickets for the game on Saturday. Would you care to come as my guest?*

HOW IT WORKS

Selling is very close in many ways to courtship. Or maybe it is the other way around. Whatever, the Courtship Close works by using many of the methods that young men use to woo young women. Or women men, or men men. Or whatever. Courtship varies around the world and even around one country. So, know the triggers and press the right buttons and the other person will be flattered enough to buy you, hook, line and sinker.

Customer-care Close

After a meeting that does not result in a close, call up the customer as the Customer Service Manager. Explain that it is a normal follow-up call to check the quality and customer-orientation of the sales staff.

Ask about the appearance, courtesy and knowledge levels of the salesperson. This, in itself, is highly valuable information.

Then ask for reasons why they did not buy. This gives you objection information you can then address. For example, you can say that because they have been so helpful, you (as the manager) can offer an extra discount.

- *Hello, Mr. X. I'm the Customer Service Manager at XYZ. I believe you spoke with one of our sales representatives on Monday. We have a strong customer service policy in the company and regularly check to ensure we are helping you at every step of the way. Could you take a couple of minutes to help answer a few questions?*
- *Mr. X, I can understand why it seemed expensive. Well, as you have been so helpful, I can offer you an extra discount today.*

HOW IT WORKS

The Customer-care Close shows that you care about the person, building trust and creating a bond between the customer and the Service Manager. It also gives you information that you can use to both improve your sales technique and also handle objections in this sale.

Doubt Close

Express doubt either about the product or the readiness of the person for the product but make this a relatively weak and easily challenged statement.

Pause to let the person disagree, which a contradicting person will almost certainly do. If they do not challenge your doubt, then smoothly continue with a summary of everything so far.

- *I don't know if this product is the right thing for you.*
- *I'm not sure if you're ready for this. Although it does ... (review benefits).*
- *Although most people do not know how to use these, perhaps you can...*

HOW IT WORKS

The Doubt Close works by pre-empting their doubting thoughts. If you echo these thoughts, it saves them from having to think the same thoughts. When they accept these, they will begin to trust you and hence will be ready to accept suggestions of other things to think.

Economic close

Focus on the overall economic situation, showing how the cost is less by considering certain factors.

Show how buying a larger quantity gives volume discounts, reducing the unit cost.

Show how buying alternatives has hidden costs.

Structure deals for them that will cost less overall.

Talk about the longer-term costs.

- *You get more for your money in the family-sized box.*
- *Yes, it is cheaper in the next town, but it will cost you more in travel to get there. And you've already spent money to travel here.*
- *You can buy on credit card, but our financing system has lower interest rates.*
- *This model, sir, is much better value.*

HOW IT WORKS

Many people focus solely on price, and this plays directly to their concern by showing you are trying to save them money. By doing this, you also gain trust and may be able to sell them more. Even those who are not so concerned about price will have it as an issue at some level, and again you will impress them by taking up this cause for them.

Embarrassment Close

Manoeuvre them into a position where *not* buying would embarrass them.

Dissuade them from buying cheap (rather than 'less expensive') options by pointing out that they are cheap, low quality, etc. and that more expensive options are much better value.

Tell stories of cheapskates who make 'false savings' with the cheap options.

Sell to the people they are with, so the other person would have to disappoint their friends, family, etc. by not buying.

Appeal to their sense of important and affluence.

- *This is the cheapest option. This one, however, is much better value.*
- *Hello young man, do you like this? ... Well, madam, I think he's made a choice!*
- *Not many people can afford this one.*

HOW IT WORKS

The Embarrassment Close appeals to emotions such as pride. It uses the Alignment principle to get people to align their buying actions with their self-image of kind, affluent, etc.

It works particularly well if the other person is in a social situation where the embarrassment would be particularly strong, from a group of peers to a person of the opposite sex.

Young men, perhaps unsurprisingly, are particularly susceptible to the Embarrassment Close.

Emotion Close

Play to their emotions, deliberately evoking specific emotions. Find if they respond more to positive or negative emotions and act accordingly.

If in doubt, go for positive emotions - these are usually better.

- *If you took this home now, how would you feel?*
- *Does holding that make you feel good?*
- *People who do not buy this invariably feel bad later.*

HOW IT WORKS

The Emotion Close works because all decisions are based on emotions. Even if you go through a logical thought process, the final step is always emotional.

Empathy Close

Empathize with them. Feel what they feel. Walk a mile in their shoes. Understand their situation completely.

Then, when they are empathizing back, *you* decide like they would decide.

You can even talk about yourself, using 'I' instead of 'you'.

Also empathize with the product you are selling and bring this into the equation. Be a matchmaker in bringing this great product to a worthy customer.

- *I completely understand...and it makes so much sense to me to do this now.*
- *You know, this solution works so well for me.*

HOW IT WORKS

The Empathy Close works by first harmonizing yourself with them and then, when you feel what it is like for them to close, they naturally come along with you.

Done well, you will close at the exactly the right moment and for exactly the right reasons for them, and they will come back again and again.

The Empathy close is also called the Love Close.

If you love the product you are selling and love your customers, you will be a truly great salesperson.

Exclusivity Close

Explain how not everybody is allowed to buy this item and that some form of 'qualification' is needed.

If they do not meet the criteria, you can quietly 'let them' buy as a special favour.

- *This discount is for local residents only. Do you live in the town? ... Yes, of course I can see you have shopping bags from Rio's Store.*
- *This is a membership special, sir. You get 20% off if you're member of our club -- it's very cheap to join.*
- *To start this high-powered course, you have to have completed the introduction training. Shall I sign you up for that first?*
- *There is normally a 5% discount for regular customers. Don't tell the boss but I'll give it to you if you can pay cash (he won't find out then).*

HOW IT WORKS

When we are told we cannot have something, our sense of control is offended, so we are motivated to take control.

When we find we qualify for something, then our sense of identity is boosted as we gain a sense of belonging to a 'special group' (and which makes our satisfaction with the purchase higher).

Give-take close

Offer them something attractive, then retract the offer, taking it away.

Then make them work to get it back. You might find they're desperate enough to pay full price.

- *Here's what you were looking for. Oh, hang on, it's already been reserved for someone else. ... Well, if you want to pay cash now, maybe I could order a replacement in time for the other customer.*
- *Ladies and gentlemen, would you pay 20 for this potato peeler? Of course, you would, and many have, but I'm not going to let you have it. Not yet. Now I'm going to add this utility knife and this apple corer, both worth 15 each and only ask 25 for the whole lot. Now I've only a few left, who's going to take them? Thank you, madam, Yes sir, one's for you...*

HOW IT WORKS

When a person sees something desirable, they start to psychologically close on it. Even paying attention creates a weak sense of ownership. When you take the product away, you affect the person's need for a sense of control with the result that they will likely fight back, figuratively trying to take back what is 'theirs'.

The scarcity principle says that people want what is scarce, and the scarcer it is, the more they want it.

Handshake Close

As you make a closing offer, extend your hand for a handshake. Smile and nod as if the deal is done. Look expectantly. If necessary, raise your eyebrows slightly.

- *(Extending hand) So, are you ready now to do the deal today?*
- *(Extending hand) We have a deal?*
- *(Grasp their hand) Well done. You've got a good deal today.*

HOW IT WORKS

When you offer your hand to somebody in greeting, they will automatically feel obliged to shake your hand in return, often doing this without really thinking.

When they do shake your hand, they may realize that they are also agreeing to the close. Most people will not then feel able to retract their agreement.

Humour Close

Get them amused by telling a joke or otherwise making witty remarks. Then either go for a relaxed close with another closing technique or weave closure into the joke.

This is particularly useful when they are tense for some reason.

Beware of politically incorrect humour unless you are sure it will be effective.

Self-deprecating humour is often a safe bet and shows you to be confident and likable.

- *This carpet was personally woven by the Queen of Sheba.*
- *Oh, go on. It'll make both our wives very happy.*
- *If you don't buy this now, I'll be told to go and stand in the corner!*
- *I'd better not sit down in case the boss sees me.*

HOW IT WORKS

Relaxed and happy people are less likely to object.

When you make someone laugh, they will like you more. And we are more likely to buy from people we like.

Never-the-best-time Close

When people are procrastinating or dithering over whether they should buy now or buy later, show them that delaying will either get them no advantage or may even be to their disadvantage.

Talk about what they will miss by not having it over the coming period.

Give examples of people who waited for the best moment, which never came.

- *If you leave it until next year, you'll have one year less to enjoy it.*
- *The best time to buy is when you need it -- which I'd say is now, wouldn't you?*
- *My friend spent his whole life looking for the perfect partner.*

HOW IT WORKS

Close works by reframing delaying tactics as value-destroying procrastination

No-hassle Close

Make completing the deal so completely easy for them that any thought that might put them off is not there.

Fill in all forms for them. Do all the paperwork.

Include delivery, installation and setup.

- *I've filled in all the paperwork and all you need is to sign here.*
- *It will be delivered Tuesday, when you are in, and fully in-*

stalled by qualified fitters.
HOW IT WORKS

The No-hassle Close works by being so simple and easy for the other person that any anticipated difficulty or hassle that may be holding them back is blown away.

It also encourages them to return the favour as an exchange for your help with the completion.

Puppy Close

There are a number of variants of Puppy Close.

Give them the product to try out. If possible, let them take it home. Like a puppy, it should sell itself.

Be charming and cute, just like a puppy dog.

Flatter them. Be very nice. Act something like a good child who deserves a reward.

Another variant is to frame what you are selling in the same cute and fluffy light.

- *Can I leave it with you for the week?*
- *It would be so nice if you bought one from me today.*

You know, I just love meeting people like you who know what they want now.

- *Oh, go on, spoil yourself.*
- *Just look at it. Isn't it so loveable?*
- *Would you like to hold it? Doesn't it feel SOOO good?*

HOW IT WORKS

The Puppy Close, when you give them the item to try out, works by the investment principle, whereas they spend time with it they grow closer to it as they associate their identity with it.

The Puppy Close, when you are acting in a cute way, works

by appeal principle, where you appeal to their kind and gentle nature. By framing the other person as good and kind (with which, of course, they agree), you also invoke the consistency principle, where they then feel obliged to act in alignment with the way you have described them (and they have accepted as an accurate and true description).

Acting in a child role is playing the Parent-Child game from Transactional Analysis. Where you act as a needy and deserving child, you invoke the Nurturing Parent in them.

Quality Close

Emphasize quality over other factors, particularly price.
Talk about how other people will be impressed by the quality of the product.
Talk about how quality products last longer, wear less, require less maintenance, etc.
'Sell on Quality, not on Price'

EXAMPLES
- *For a one-off payment you get non-stop quality.*
- *The quality of this shows really who you are.*
- *This will last forever.*
- *Once you try this, you will never want another brand.*
- *This product is far more reliable.*

HOW IT WORKS

The Quality Close works by appealing either to the other person's vanity or to their sense of longer-term value. For vanity, you are associating their identity with 'quality'. For value, you are reframing price across time.

Rational Close

Use logic and reason to persuade. Show them evidence that the product works well and that other customers were satisfied. Leverage science and irrefutable proof. Explain reasonably why buying is the right choice.

With care, you can construct a powerful argument that uses a traditional and proven structure for persuasion.

- *Well now, we've gone through all you need, and the product meets these well, right? ... And the price is good, true? ... Now is there anything else that would stop you buying today? ... No? So, let's do the paperwork.*
- *Do you want a carpet that will wear well with your children and your dogs? That will repel the dirt and stay fresh, even in doorways? This product uses a scientifically proven formula that lets us offer you a ten-year anti-wear guarantee.*

HOW IT WORKS

This approach works simply by using rational reasoning that calls upon logic and science. As we are brought up in a social and educational system that defines science and reason to be correct, such an approach is powerfully persuasive.

Some people decide by thinking and other more by feeling. This approach works well with many people, though it is most effective with the thinking decision-makers.

Repetition Close

Achieve the close by repeating a closing action several times. Show them the product, then other products, then come back to the product, ... and repeat these three or four times.

Tell them several reasons why they should buy.

Ask several questions that remind them about the product.

Tell them about several different other people who bought the product.

When they refuse, go back to the product several times.

- *Look at this...you could try that...but this is good too...and another...but this...*
- *I know you're not going to buy, but I just want to show you one more thing...*

HOW IT WORKS

The Repetition Close works because many people need to repeat things a few times before they 'get it'. In a shoe shop, for example, they may have to pick up and put down a pair of shoes three times before they decide to buy.

Many people have a certain number of times they need to repeat things before they achieve personal closure. If you can find this number (often around three or four), then you know how many times to repeat your close.

Repetition is a very fundamental pattern that affects us in primal ways.

Retrial Close

When things are not going your way, and perhaps when your customer has already said 'no' (and perhaps a number of times), then seek to reset the clock by obviating any past decisions through new data or proving that decisions were shaky or incorrect.

- *I have looked deeper into this and found that we were using the wrong information.*
- *I'm sorry but I lost my notes from last time. Can we go over*

> *a few things again?*
> - *After talking with Jan, it seems the requirements have changed...*

HOW IT WORKS

The Retrial Close works in the same way that a retrial is forced in a court of law, where evidence that was accepted in the original trial is proved to be unsafe.

Perhaps it seems it is not so much a closing technique as a unclosing technique? The actual closure is in the decision to open the negotiations again.

Reversal Close

Act as if you do not want them to buy the product.

When they are objecting, just take the product back and put it on the shelf (or worse, give it to another salesperson).

Suddenly remember that this is the last one and it was reserved by someone else.

When they object to you 'deciding for them', do not give in easily. Let yourself be persuaded by them, and only take the product out again when you have a much firmer interest or commitment.

This is particularly useful if they seem to have a contrary nature.

How strongly you do this reversal depends on how much they pull back. It's a bit like fishing - too much tugging and the fish will swim away, whilst a delicate touch will bring the fish inevitably to the shore.

You can also use the idea of reversal in other ways, for example to elicit objections by asking them why they would *not* buy from you.

- *This is clearly not for you. Thank you for coming in today, anyway.*
- *Oh no! This one was reserved for another customer and we have no more.*
- *I really don't think this is your style.*
- *I'm not going to get it out again unless you are sure this is the one for you.*

HOW IT WORKS

The Reversal Close works by causing reactance, where your autonomous actions cause them to take an opposite stance.

It can also be useful when they are suspicious of you trying to sell them something. By refusing to sell, you appear to be on their side or, at the very least, you will have broken their stereotype of a typical salesperson.

Selective-deafness Close

Also known as the Selective-deafness close, you ignore anything that the other person says, or does that does not lead you towards a close. Well, not so much ignore it as act as if it has not been said (you actually think hard about why they are saying what they do and seek ways to lead them away from it).

- *(they say it is too expensive) - Won't it look great in your house?*
- *(they start to walk away) - Just look at this feature!*
- *(they ask about things you do not have) - Would you like a cup of coffee?*

HOW IT WORKS

The Selective-deafness Close works by the principle that you get what you talk about. If their attention is on why they cannot buy, then they are likely to not buy.

It also is related to the locus of control. If you are talking about what they want, you are on their agenda and they are in control. What you want is for them to *think* that they are in control, but they are actually walking down the path you control.

Shopping List Close

First elicit the buyer's needs, including product features and other elements such as service levels, usability and so on.

Write these down and verify with the buyer that this is what they want. Of course, ensure that what you write down is something that you can supply.

Then show the customer the items on the list. The 'shopping list' close is done as you check off each item as you show it.

If you can't cover everything, make sure the things you can't cover are (a) few and (b) relatively unimportant.

- *OK. So what you want is a yellow shirt that can been hand-washed and which is going to last for a long time. Here's the ideal thing from our 'everlasting' range: Yellow (check), Hand washable -- see the label? (Check), and everlasting means at least five years -- guaranteed.*
- *Here's your list. Let's see if we've covered it. 200db (check), noise reduction (check), onsite service (check), ... That's it. We've got it all. So what do you say?*

HOW IT WORKS

The Shopping List close works first by convincing the buyer that the list itself is all that they need, which is done by careful questioning and writing in a form where the seller can demonstrate compliance.

The convincing part of the close is in the way that you check off each item. The effect is that each time you do this, it causes the buyer to experience a psychological close. The repetition is like a series of hammer-blows that create a strong final close.

The completed list is also means that the buyer cannot have any objections.

Summary Close

Summarize the list of benefits that the other person will receive, telling them the full extent of what they are getting for their money.

Make it sound impressive, using full phrases and attractive words.

Go into detail, separating out as many sub-items and features as you can.

But also fit the description into a reasonable space of time. You goal is to impress them with what they are getting, not to bore them with excessive detail.

- *So as well as the basic product, you are getting free delivery, a five-day exchange assurance plus our comprehensive guarantee.*
- *This comes in an easy-carry box and includes a remote control, with batteries included, of course!*

HOW IT WORKS

The Summary Close works by repeating what has already been agreed. Putting it all together makes it seem like an even bigger package.

Testimonial Close

Use a happy customer to convince the other person.

Show them letters from happy customers. Have the letters on the wall.

If you are using the name of the happy customer, make sure they agree to you doing this. Otherwise you will have to use an anonymous reference, such as 'satisfied customer from Birmingham' or 'major airline'.

Persuade happy customers act as references, that the other person can either call up or they can visit. Reward the happy customer with appropriate thanks, which may range from a simple letter to a small present to a discount. Be very careful here to ensure the customer feels valued and does not feel they are being bribed.

- *I regularly receive letters from happy customers. Here are a few.*
- *XYZ Corporation are regular customers.*
- *We have several customers who are happy to act as reference sites for us. Would you like me to arrange a visit for you?*

HOW IT WORKS

The Testimonial Close works by providing evidence from a credible source. If they do not trust you, they are much more likely to trust someone who is similar to them.

Think About It Close

After you've said what you can, give the person a little time to think about what you have told and shown them.

Don't leave them for too long (a couple of minutes is often

enough) and preferably go where you can keep an eye on them. A way of handling this is to ask them how long they need.

When you return, watch their body language to see if they are showing signs of being ready to buy. If necessary, use an assumptive method to nudge them over the edge.

- *I can see you're carefully thinking about. I'm going to step outside for a couple of minutes so you can decide in your own time.*
- *How long would you like to think about it? Can I get you a cup of coffee whilst you decide?*
- *Perhaps you'd like to talk about it together. Why don't you sit in the car and see how it feels. Take as long as you like -- I'll be here.*

HOW IT WORKS

Not everyone decides quickly and many, and if pressed many will back away or react against the sales methods being used.

Decision-making is often a complex thought process pros and cons are weighed up and the person may not decide until they have gone through this process. This is particularly common in sales which involve significant money or other commitment.

Sometimes it just takes a little time to sink in. You have given them a lot of information which they need to process it and fit it in with their current models of the world.

Of course, there is a danger when the person thinks about it that they will say no. Depending on the sales context this could a bad or good thing. People who buy only because they are pressured are unlikely to return or recommend you. On the other hand this final 'soft sell' stage may well convince them that it is they who are in control and so will make the decision to buy.

The Think About It close is in some ways a form of Assumptive Close, as you are assuming that all they need is time to decide.

Trial Close

A Trial Close is not a normal 'closing technique' but a test to determine whether the person is ready to close.

Use it after a presentation or after you have made a strong selling point. Use it when you have answered objections.

The Trial Close may use other closing techniques or may be a more tentative question.

Ask 'If...' questions.

Ask questions that assume they have already bought the product.

When you have asked the Trial Close question, as with most other closes, <u>be quiet</u>, watching and listening carefully for their response.

'ABC' is a common abbreviation: Always Be Closing. It means that you should always be heading towards a close, although you must also be careful about over-doing this. If people are nowhere near ready to buy, this will just annoy them.

- *It looks like you really like this. Is that true?*
- *If you took it home, would you be proud to own this?*
- *Do you prefer the larger or smaller version?*
- *How would it look on the shelf back at home?*

HOW IT WORKS

The Trial Close works by putting the idea of closure into the person's mind. Their response will tell you whether they are ready or not.

Valuable Customer Close

Find a reason to show that the customer is of particular value to you, and then offer them a special, one-off discount. You may, of course, start with a particularly high price (that reflects the quality of your product, of course).

Say their installation will be a model example that you want to photograph as a reference site for use in brochures and offer a discount in return.

Say that you need one more sale to complete your quota for the month/quarter and that you will offer an extra discount to get the sale.

Call back later as Sales Manager and say the customer is so valuable; you are able to offer an extra discount.

- *You are clearly well-connected in the area. Tell you what, I'm going to offer you an extra discount because I believe that you will be so impressed you will tell all of your friends.*
- *Hello, I'm The area Sales Manager for XYZ. Your house is in a prime position and I'm prepared to cut out the sales person (don't tell him!) so we can reduce the price and get you on board.*
- The Valuable Customer Close works by flattering the customer into believing that the discount that you are offering is more than they would normally get, and hence offers unusually good value.

Yes-set Close

Ask them several questions where the answer is easy to answer and is 'yes'. Then tag on the question at the end for which you *really* want the answer 'yes'.

The minimum set is usually three questions. You also do not want to over-do this, so either space out the questions or limit the number (although one research showed that eight yeses were needed overall before closure).

Encourage them to say yes by nodding your head gently as you talk with them.

If you need to hide the question, you can bury it amongst other questions.

- *Do you like coming to shop here?*
- *Is it easy to find us?*
- *Did this product catch your eye?*
- *Are you ready to buy it now?*
- *Will you want to take delivery next week?*

HOW IT WORKS

The Yes-set Close works by setting up a repetitive pattern of 'yes' answers that gets the other person into a habitual response. When the pattern is established and they are automatically answering 'yes', then the question that you really want 'yes' to is slipped in.

Many people also do not particularly like to answer 'no' as they believe that it is impolite.

OBJECTION-HANDLING

When a salesperson demonstrates a feature, talks about a benefit or uses a sales closing technique, their customer may well respond in the negative sense, giving excuses or otherwise heading away from the sale. The response to this is to handle these objections. This is 'objection-handling'.

OBJECTION-HANDLING PROCESS

This is an overall process to handle objections. See the objection-handling page for a list of methods for the detail of handling objections.

1. Listen

Stop! Do not try to jump in at the beginning - this may cause further objection. When you interrupt them, *you* are objecting to their objection. If you refuse to listen, then their next steps may well be towards the door.

Use active listening methods, nodding and physically showing interest.

They are trying to tell you something that will help you sell to them, which is a gift from them to you. If you do not listen, then their next step may well be towards the door.

2. Question

As appropriate, ask some questions. This not only shows you are interested in them, but it also gives you more information with which to make the sale. As you question them, watch carefully for body language that gives you more information about what they are thinking and feeling.

Remember that this is not an interrogation, and that giving

them the 'third degree' will turn them off. So, keep your questions light and relevant.

You might also tip the bucket at this time, asking them if there are any more concerns (=objections) that they have, and which, if you can resolve them, you might gain a close.

It is not always necessary to ask questions. Be deliberate about what you are doing if you do.

3. Think

Now before you dive into objection-handling, think! What methods will work best with them? Should you take a direct and confrontational approach, or should you use the soft-soap to finesse the situation? Or maybe you should put it off to another day (but only if you can be sure that you can return to the selling situation).

Thinking is a good thing where you are adding a little pause into the proceedings, thus demonstrating how you are taking their objection seriously.

4. Handle

This stage may sometimes only be a few seconds after they object, or it may require more time in the previous three steps. Now, when you are ready, use the objection-handling method that you believe will work best. Or make up your own. You are under no obligation to try and force-fit a method where it is unlikely to work.

5. Check

Finally, check to find out whether your objection-handling worked! Ask if you have answered their question. Ask if there are any more concerns. As necessary, handle outstanding objections.

Then go for the close.

LACE

Objections happen. If you perform the sales or persuasion process well, you will succeed in seriously reducing the number of objections, but they may still happen.

Objections can be transformed into an opportunity. For example, you can increase understanding of the other person's circumstance and to get closer to them, building a more trusting relationship.

Listen

Before you can act on the objection, it helps a great deal if you can understand properly not only the objection but also the thought and emotion behind it.

Find the objection

First, listen some more. Ask questions that elicit the background and detail of the objection. Listen not only to the objection but to the emotion behind it. Seek to 'read between the lines'.

The objection as stated may well be a cover for the real objection. Probe for more detail. Ask 'what else' and 'how come'.

Find remaining objections

Find out whether there are any other objections. Ask 'Is there anything else'. Tip the bucket. This can cause you more work now and it may seem that it is better to let sleeping dogs lie. But if you do not do so, then when you get towards what you hope is closure, they may easily pop up to frustrate you once again.

Accept

Once you have discovered the objection, the next stage is to acknowledge not only the objection but the person, too.

Accept the person

First and throughout, accept the person. Accept that they have a right to object. Accept that you have not fully understood them.

You do not do this by saying 'I accept you' or anything like this. The simplest way is through your attitude. Objecting can be a scary act, and people can fear your reaction. By not reacting negatively, by accepting the objection, you also accept the person.

By accepting the person, you build both their trust and their sense of identity with you. You also set up a exchange dynamic where they feel a sense of obligation to repay your acceptance.

Accept the objection

Accepting the objection means understanding how it is reasonable, at least from their current viewpoint for them to object to what you may believe is an excellent offer.

It also means accepting the work that addressing the objection will require of you. Objections can be frustrating and if you object to the objection, you will have a mutual stalemate.

Commit

Now it is time to get serious. With the increased understanding and trust, you have an ideal opportunity for a trial close.

Get their commitment

Get a commitment from them such that if you can satisfactorily address their objections, they will agree with you and make the purchase.

This is also a good method of identifying further objections. If they say no, then loop back and elicit these. Eventually, they will run out of objections. If you can address these, it's in the bag.

Make your commitment

This is also the point where you may well be making a commitment to them, to resolve their objections. This may be difficult and cost you in various ways, from calling in favours from other people to putting in additional effort.

The decision you have here, is 'Is it worth it?' Persuasion is often an exchange, and you always at liberty to back out.

Explicit action

Now it is time to address the objections, to take explicit action on the commitments made.

There are two types of objection: real ones and accidental ones. Accidental objections are where the objection is due to a misunderstanding. Misunderstandings are usually easy to address, with an apology and an explanation.

Real objections take work, but if they can be resolved, you've got the sale!

Persuade your way through

Persuading your way through an objection means working to change the way they view the objections. You can wear them down such that they no longer view the objection as being worth pursuing. You can also change the way they view them more positively such that they have an 'aha' experience that leads them to perceive the objection as being no longer important.

Concede your way through

You can also concede your way through, giving in and effectively buying their commitment. If they object to the price, you can always lower it. If they don't want it now, you can come back next week.

Concession can be both a useful approach, especially if you are in a hurry, and a threat. If you give them an inch, then they may want to take a mile. But this is not necessarily so, and a prepared concession strategy can pay dividends.

Tip the bucket

'Tipping the bucket' is a simple, but perhaps counter-intuitive thing to do when the other person objects.

What you do is to ask for *more* objections. In fact, you ask for all the objections you can get, thus 'tipping the bucket' of objections that they have been thinking about.

The advantage of this is that you now know all the reasons they have for not buying and can decide what to do about them.

- *Are there any other reasons why you are not yet ready?*
- *What else is stopping you from buying today?*
- *It sounds like you have several problems here. What else is on your mind?*

HOW IT WORKS

Tipping the bucket not only gives you the advantage of knowing their reasons not to buy, it also shows that you are interested in them personally and want to solve the problems that they have.

This builds trust and may enable you to reframe the situation as joint-problem-solving rather than you trying to sell and them fending you off with objections.

Types of objection

There are many types of objection. Here are a few of the main ones. If you can classify how they object, then you are on the first step to handling the objection.

Need

They say that they do not need your product or service for some reason or another, or perhaps have a need that you cannot satisfy.

EXAMPLES
- *I have one of those already.*
- *My car works just fine thank you.*
- *I have no space for anymore.*
- *Sorry, I just don't want it.*

Price

The objections here are about the price of the product.

EXAMPLES
- *How much??*
- *I have already spent my budget for the month.*
- *Your competitors sell a better product for less money.*
- *I could get it cheaper on the web.*
- *I didn't realize that service was not included.*

Features

They object to some element of what you are selling, whether it is aspects of a service or details of a product.

EXAMPLES
- *I don't like that style. It looks rather modern for me.*
- *It does not have the latest gadgets.*

- *The guarantee is only six months.*
- *It is far too big.*
- *It is not good enough quality.*

Time

In this, the objection is around time, such as the person not being ready to buy.

EXAMPLES

- *I don't know. I need to think about it.*
- *I won't have the money until next month.*
- *I am moving next year, maybe then.*
- *I need to talk to my manager first.*

Source

They question the source of the product, often its credibility. This may include questions about you, too.

EXAMPLES

- *I do not know you from Adam. I prefer to buy from people I know.*
- *I saw a report about how badly your company treated its workers.*
- *How will I know if you are around to service this in five years?*

Boomerang method

When people object, turn them around by using what they say to prove that they are wrong.

Use their own arguments like a boomerang, so they go around in a circle and come back to persuade them.

- *Yes, it is expensive, but I don't think you would want to buy*

- *your wife a cheap present.*
- *Indeed, the house does need work, but as you said, you are very good at Do-It-Yourself work.*
- *Certainly, if you do not have the money today then we can arrange it all for tomorrow.*

HOW IT WORKS

By using what they say, you are saying that they are right. And when you attach what you want to what they say, then by association, what you want is right.

OBJECTION CHUNKING

You can take more higher, more general viewpoint or a more detailed focus.

Chunking up (also called *Helicoptering*) lets you see more and understand the big picture. When you chunk up, specific issues seem small and insignificant. My worries about a scratch on a car is nothing in comparison with world peace.

You can expand the pie, showing them how they are getting not only the basic product, but other things as well. You can add widgets and warranties. You can add emotions like the added peace of mind they will have from your product.

Chunking down drills into the detail, highlighting and addressing significant concerns. It also distracts attention away from more difficult concerns in other areas.

You can reduce the apparent size of the objection, for example by changing a dislike of town into a dislike of a neighbourhood or just a street.

- *Let's look at the big picture. What do you really want achieve by using this?*
- *That's interesting. Tell me more about that...*
- *How does your CEO think about this?*
- *Tell you what. Let's get one of your engineers to consider the situation.*

HOW IT WORKS

Taking a different perspective has a dual effect, first of reframing to create a different attention and a new understanding, and secondly of distracting from what might be a difficult issue to resolve.

Deflection

Avoid handling an objection by deflecting it such that it does not hold up the proceedings.

Listen to it. Show understanding of the concerns. Then carry on as if nothing had happened.

Say that you will come back to it later. Maybe you won't have to. Give an excuse, such as not having information or having to talk to somebody else later.

- *Yes, I see what you mean...mmm...Now let me show you the range of finishes you can have...*
- *Good point. Can I come back to that later?...thanks...Now what I was saying was...*
- *Yes, I've got some information about that back at the office somewhere. Can we carry on now? ...*

HOW IT WORKS

By accepting their objection, you are accepting them as a person, and the additional harmony and rapport created may be enough to overcome the objection.

Refusing to answer their objections now may also be a power play, where you are demonstrating authority and control over the situation. If you can get away with it, they may cede more power to you.

Feel, felt, found

First empathies with them, telling them that you understand how they *feel*.

Then tell them about somebody who *felt* the same way.

Then tell them how that other person *found* that things were not so bad and that when they did what you want the buyer to do they found that it was actually a very good thing to do.

- *I understand you feel about that. Many others have felt the same way. And what they have found is that....*
- *I know how you feel that it looks rough. I had a person in here yesterday who felt the same when they first looked at it. But when they tried it on they found that it was so comfortable.*
- *You know I feel the same about products when I first see them. I felt the same recently when I bought a new car. But when I took it home for the weekend, I found that everyone I know was so envious.*

HOW IT WORKS

By empathizing with how they *feel*, you are building harmony with them to create rapport. When you talk about how somebody else *felt*, you move the focus to a more objective place which they are likely to trust more. This also makes them a part of a group such that they do not feel alone. When they are attached to that group, then you move the whole group by telling how the person in the group changed their mind. The buyer, being attached to the group, should change their mind at the same time.

Handling objections with humour

When they object, do not respond with negative emotions such as anger or frustration.

Defuse the tension with gentle humour, maybe feigning shock or otherwise poking fun at yourself.

Be careful about making them the object of humour. It can be done, but you need to be sure first that they will not be offended.

- *Oh no! What will we do! (smiling)*
- *Well I think this car would be very sad to see you go home without it.*
- *I think I've lost my touch. (looking at hands with puzzled expression)*

HOW IT WORKS

When you receive objections, it can be very frustrating, and it is very easy for these emotions to leak out. By reframing the situation with gentle humour, you can show that you are not offended by their refusal.

Remember that they, too, may find objecting embarrassing and uncomfortable, with the result that they may well want to get away from you (and the embarrassment) as soon as possible.

Justification

Rather than fight the objection, justify why it is reasonable.

Tell them how you have deliberately made what you are selling this way for a particular reason.

If they complain about price, tell them the product is built for a superior market.

If they complain about quality, tell them that this is to allow you to charge a very low price.

- *Yes, the car is expensive, but it is a rare import and cost a lot to bring over here.*
- *I know it is not new, but it will give your image depth, mak-*

ing you look more established.
- *It is large, which is why most people who buy it find that visitors notice it at once.*

HOW IT WORKS

When people object, they often are saying that what you are offering is somehow unfair or wrong. If you can subsequently show that it is fair and reasonable, then they no longer have reason to object.

LAARC

This is another acronym to help you remember things to do when you are handling objections from your customer.

Listen
First listen to what they have to say. Avoid the temptation to jump in at the first moment you can. Wait patiently for them to complete what they are saying.

Acknowledge
When you have heard them, acknowledge the person, their right to object, the validity of their objection. If you do not do this, they may take your response personally and the conversation will descend into a failing duel.

Assess
Having listened to and acknowledged the person, assess the situation. This may mean asking various questions to probe for further detail. You know when you have completed the assessment stage when you can fully empathize with the person's objection.

Respond
Only when you have a proper grasp of the objection should you start to respond. Structure this carefully, perhaps using one of the objection-handling techniques here.

Always be careful to ensure you respond fully and adequately to the objections given. Beware of straying off the path of responding to the objection or else you may end up creating more objections.

Confirm

Finally, check with the other person that they have understood your response and that it addresses their concerns.

If the other person still has the objection, repeat the loop. See if you have listened well enough in the first place. Check that you have assessed their situation correctly. Ensure that the response fully and adequately addresses their concerns.

Objection Writing

When they object, tip the bucket to get all remaining objections, writing these down as you go on a clean page of paper.

Then show it to the other person and verify that if you address these, then there are no reasons for them not to buy.

Then, as you handle each one, cross it out. You can ask the person before this (*'So, we have addressed this. Can I cross this out now?'*)

A variant of this is to summarize the objections into one word or a short phrase. Thus you write down 'price', 'size' and so on. This allows you to reframe slightly what they are saying.

How it works

Writing things down is useful for a visual thinker. It also moved the problem onto the external, objective sheet of paper (from their subjective thinking). And then it allows you to cross it out. The act of crossing it out causes closure, on eliminating the objection.

Pre-empting objections

Tell them about a possible objection before they object. Then handle the objection so it cannot be brought up again.

Make the objection rather weak and the handling rather strong.

Tell them stories of other people who objected and then looked foolish.

I had one person didn't like the shade, but then they had not realized that this was the latest fashion.

You might find this expensive, but we can find the right deal.

HOW IT WORKS

If you answer the objection before they bring it out, then they are unable to voice the objection without appearing to not have heard you.

Reprioritize objections

When they have a priority, which is stopping them from buying from you, find ways of changing the priority.

Explore the criteria they are using to decide. Probe to find how important each criterion is.

Appeal to their values, which include a system of prioritization.

Reframe their arguments so they naturally change priority.

At the same time or alternatively, increase other priorities that will lead to them buying from you.

You are very loyal to your current supplier, but should you be more loyal to your family?

You are right, price is important. But how much more important is quality to you?

A big picture would look nice, but with smaller pictures you can show more of them.

HOW IT WORKS

When evaluating between different choices, we use different criteria and different weighting of those criteria. We also get fixated on particular solutions and forget about other criteria. If you can change criteria, change weights or remind the other person of forgotten criteria then you can get them to reprioritize.

www.ingramcontent.com/pod-product-compliance
Lightning Source LLC
Chambersburg PA
CBHW060840220526
45466CB00003B/1177